Field Guides to Finding a New Career

Outdoor Careers

The Field Guides to Finding a New Career series

Field Guides
to Finding a
New Career

Outdoor Careers

By Amanda Kirk

Checkmark Books®

An imprint of Infobase Publishing

Field Guides to Finding a New Career: Outdoor Careers

Copyright © 2009 by Print Matters, Inc.

Checkmark Books
An imprint of Infobase Publishing
132 West 31st Street
New York NY 10001

Library of Congress Cataloging-in-Publication Data

Kirk, Amanda.
    Field guides to finding a new career : outdoor careers / by Amanda Kirk. p. cm.
    Includes bibliographical references and index.
    ISBN-13: 978-0-8160-7603-1 (hardcover : alk. paper)
    ISBN-10: 0-8160-7603-0 (hardcover : alk. paper)
    ISBN-13: 978-0-8160-7627-7 (pbk. : alk. paper)
    ISBN-10: 0-8160-7627-8 (pbk. : alk. paper) 1. Outdoor life—Vocational guidance—
United States. 2. Occupations—United States. I. Title.
    HF5382.5.U5K52 2009
    331.7020973—dc22

                                                    2009000601

You can find Ferguson on the World Wide Web at http://www.fergpubco.com

Produced by Print Matters, Inc.
Text design by A Good Thing, Inc.
Illustrations by Molly Crabapple
Cover design by Takeshi Takahashi

Printed in the United States of America

Bang PMI 10 9 8 7 6 5 4 3 2 1

This book is printed on acid-free paper.

Contents

Introduction: Finding a New Career

Today, changing jobs is an accepted and normal part of life. In fact, according to the Bureau of Labor Statistics, Americans born between 1957 and 1964 held an average of 9.6 jobs from the ages of 18 to 36. The reasons for this are varied: To begin with, people live longer and healthier lives than they did in the past and accordingly have more years of active work life. However, the economy of the twenty-first century is in a state of constant and rapid change, and the workforce of the past does not always meet the needs of the future. Furthermore, fewer and fewer industries provide bonuses such as pensions and retirement health plans, which provide an incentive for staying with the same firm. Other workers experience epiphanies, spiritual growth, or various sorts of personal challenges that lead them to question the paths they have chosen.

Job instability is another prominent factor in the modern workplace. In the last five years, the United States has lost 2.6 *million jobs*; in 2005 alone, 370,000 workers were affected by mass layoffs. Moreover, because of new technology, changing labor markets, ageism, and a host of other factors, many educated, experienced professionals and skilled blue-collar workers have difficulty finding jobs in their former career tracks. Finally—and not just for women—the realities of juggling work and family life, coupled with economic necessity, often force radical revisions of career plans.

No matter how normal or accepted changing careers might be, however, the time of transition can also be a time of anxiety. Faced with the necessity of changing direction in the middle of their journey through life, many find themselves lost. Many career-changers find themselves asking questions such as: Where do I want to go from here? How do I get there? How do I prepare myself for the journey? Thankfully, the Field Guides to Finding a New Career are here to show the way. Using the language and visual style of a travel guide, we show you that reorienting yourself and reapplying your skills and knowledge to a new career is not an uphill slog, but an exciting journey of exploration. No matter whether you are in your twenties or close to retirement age, you can bravely set out to explore new paths and discover new vistas.

Though this series forms an organic whole, each volume is also designed to be a comprehensive, stand-alone, all-in-one guide to getting motivated, getting back on your feet, and getting back to work. We thoroughly discuss common issues such as going back to school, managing your household finances, putting your old skills to work in new situations, and selling yourself to potential employers. Each volume focuses on a broad career field, roughly grouped by Bureau of Labor Statistics' career clusters. Each chapter will focus on a particular career, suggesting new career paths suitable for an individual with that experience and training as well as practical issues involved in seeking and applying for a position.

Many times, the first question career-changers ask is, "Is this new path right for me?" Our self-assessment quiz, coupled with the career compasses at the beginning of each chapter, will help you to match your personal attributes to set you on the right track. Do you possess a storehouse of skilled knowledge? Are you the sort of person who puts others before yourself? Are you methodical and organized? Do you communicate effectively and clearly? Are you good at math? And how do you react to stress? All of these qualities contribute to career success—but they are not equally important in all jobs.

Many career-changers find working for themselves to be more hassle-free and rewarding than working for someone else. However, going at it alone, whether as a self-employed individual or a small-business owner, provides its own special set of challenges. Appendix A, "Going Solo: Starting Your Own Business," is designed to provide answers to many common questions and solutions to everyday problems, from income taxes to accounting to providing health insurance for yourself and your family.

For those who choose to work for someone else, how do you find a job, particularly when you have been out of the labor market for a while? Appendix B, "Outfitting Yourself for Career Success," is designed to answer these questions. It provides not only advice on résumé and self-presentation, but also the latest developments in looking for jobs, such as online resources, headhunters, and placement agencies. Additionally, it recommends how to explain an absence from the workforce to a potential employer.

Changing careers can be stressful, but it can also be a time of exciting personal growth and discovery. We hope that the Field Guides to Finding a New Career not only help you get your bearings in today's employment jungle, but set you on the path to personal fulfillment, happiness, and prosperity.

How to Use This Book

Career Compasses

Each chapter begins with a series of "career compasses" to help you get your bearings and determine if this job is right for you, based on your answers to the self-assessment quiz at the beginning of the book. Does it require a mathematical mindset? Communication skills? Organizational skills? If you're not a "people person," a job requiring you to interact with the public might not be right for you. On the other hand, your organizational skills might be just what are needed in the back office.

Destination

A brief overview, giving you and introduction to the career, briefly explaining what it is, its advantages, why it is so satisfying, its growth potential, and its income potential.

You Are Here

A self-assessment asking you to locate yourself on your journey. Are you working in a related field? Are you working in a field where some skills will transfer? Or are you doing something completely different? In each case, we suggest ways to reapply your skills, gain new ones, and launch yourself on your new career path.

Navigating the Terrain

To help you on your way, we have provided a handy map showing the stages in your journey to a new career. "Navigating the Terrain" will show you the road you need to follow to get where you are going. Since the answers are not the same for everyone and every career, we are sure to show how there are multiple ways to get to the same destination.

Organizing Your Expedition

Fleshing out "Navigating the Terrain," we give explicit directions on how to enter this new career: Decide on a destination, scout the terrain, and decide on a path that is right for you. Of course, the answers are not the same for everyone.

Landmarks

People have different needs at different ages. "Landmarks" presents advice specific to the concerns of each age demographic: early career (twenties), mid-career (thirties to forties), senior employees (fifties) and second-career starters (sixties). We address not only issues such as overcoming age discrimination, but also possible concerns of spouses and families (for instance, paying college tuition with reduced income) and keeping up with new technologies.

Essential Gear

Indispensable tips for career-changers on things such as gearing your résumé to a job in a new field, finding contacts and networking, obtaining further education and training, and how to gain experience in the new field.

Notes from the Field

Sometimes it is useful to consult with those who have gone before for insights and advice. "Notes from the Field" presents interviews with career-changers, presenting motivations and methods that you can identify with.

Further Resources

Finally, we give a list of "expedition outfitters" to provide you with further resources and trade resources.

Make the Most of Your Journey

There is a unique satisfaction to be found in a career that enables you to work outdoors and with your hands. The physical tiredness that you feel at the end of the day is different than the mental fatigue suffered after a shift spent in a cubicle in front of a computer. This is not to say that there are not plenty of lucrative, stimulating, and worthwhile careers that require you to spend your days inside. But if you are reading this volume, the siren call of the outdoors is luring you from your office into the sunlight.

In this book you will find an overview of some of the types of outdoor jobs that are available. Working outdoors usually involves interacting with the natural world in some fashion. Some jobs involve working with flora, such as farmers, foresters, plant nursery owners, or horticulturalists/garden designers. Others involve working with fauna, such as horse or dog trainers. A few outdoor careers can be hazardous, such as fishing vessel operators and ranchers, and some are ideal for the sports enthusiast, such as adventure travel guides or outdoor sports instructors. If you are physically hale and hearty, one of these outdoor careers could be right for you.

When you think of people who work outside all day long, the first jobs that come to mind are probably farmers and ranchers. They are similar occupations but farmers usually raise crops while ranchers generally raise cattle or sheep. Ranching has its own mystique and aesthetic associated with the western region of the United States. Ranchers do still exist, and you can become one, but modern ranching involves many other duties besides riding the fence line on horseback and rounding up the herd. Ranchers today often diversify their workload and supplement their incomes by offering hunting and vacation destination services on their property. Resort ranches and dude ranches are as common as old-fashioned working ranches, so there are quite a variety of ranching lifestyles to choose from if you decide that your home is on the range.

Unless it has been many decades since you have ventured out of your cubicle, you are aware that small family farms have become as rare as hen's teeth. Consolidation and economics of scale have led to the swallowing of small family farms by giant agribusiness conglomerates. However, recent movements toward organic and locally grown produce have revived the economic viability of small farms. The advent of farmers' markets, local food co-ops, and a push for giant supermarket chains such as Whole Foods to buy locally grown produce whenever possible have created new opportunities for small-scale farmers to make a living.

Forestry is another profession that has experienced a revival of sorts. Although logging of both public and private land continues, managing forested land for environmental and recreational purposes as well as for long-term profitability has created new markets for foresters. Foresters still work in national forests, helping to stop forest fires and performing other traditional tasks of the profession, but foresters are now involved in environmental education as well as ecosystem management. Urban foresters ply their trade in city parks. You might not think of foresters working in New York City, but they are there in the urban jungle—and you could be, too.

Another outdoor career that would give you the opportunity to work with trees and other plants is the plant nursery business. Gardening never goes out of style, and both commercial and residential properties need landscaping to give them life and warmth. If you have a green thumb and a bit of business acumen, your entrepreneurial spirit might move you to open your own plant nursery. Customers of your nursery could include a variety of horticulturists and garden designers. Some horticulturists spend more time in the lab than outdoors, conducting research of plant breeding and related agricultural pursuits, but there are outdoor career options. Garden designers may spend some time at a drafting table sketching out designs, but they have to get their hands dirty working with assistants to make their designs some to life. If you have a horticulture degree, or even a history of successful gardening exploits, a career in horticulture might enable you to spend more time rooting around in the dirt than in the file cabinet.

If it is the sea that calls you, a career as a fishing vessel operator will put you in the salt spray all day long. This is another profession that has changed recently. Due to overfishing, the number of commercial fishing jobs has been declining steadily and is expected to continue to decline for the foreseeable future. But do not despair if you are hoping to turn your love of boats or fishing hobby into a viable career. There will continue to be some vacancies in commercial fishing along the coasts due to retirement in this hazardous line of work. There is also a new industry of sport fishing, which has spawned due to the baby boomer generation's love of active travel. Boat owners can provide charter services for vacationing fishermen, as well as boat tours for sightseeing or onboard celebrations.

If the active vacation lifestyle appeals to you but you lack a fishing boat, you might consider working as an adventure travel guide. The baby boom generation is a large demographic, and its members are approaching retirement age with better health and more disposable income than their predecessors. These facts combined with the trend towards eco-tourism make adventure guiding a rapidly growing field. If you prefer white-water rafting, mountain climbing, exploring canyons and caves, and being active on your vacations, you are not alone. Adventure travel opportunities can be found in almost every country on Earth, so this is an ideal career option if you want to work abroad.

A great career option for you skiers, kayakers, and triathletes is outdoor sports instruction. Opportunities in this field are diverse, and one is bound to be a perfect fit for your skills and interests. If you played team sports as a kid, whether in school or with your local little league or summer camp, you know how important a good coach is to a team's success on the playing field. There are never enough coaches to accommodate all the kids who want to play outdoor sports, but at lower levels you may find this to be a labor of love rather than a viable full time career option. At schools and at higher levels of professional play, coaching can be a demanding and well-paying job. Since most sports have seasons, coaching can also be an ideal part time job. If your sport of choice is individual- rather than team-oriented, you may consider teaching it as an outdoor sports instructor. Whatever your sport, there are people who will pay you to teach it to them. It might be a challenge to make sport instruction your full time career, but it can be a suitable adjunct to a related pursuit or an off-season job or other sport.

If you think you would be happier teaching animals than people, perhaps a career as a dog or horse trainer is more suitable. If you are contemplating a change to a career involving animals, you should have some experience working with them already. These are not fields for amateurs, as someone's life or health could depend upon your expertise. As an animal trainer, you are helping to socialize an animal to live in a human environment, subduing its natural instincts and teaching it to perform on command. Safety of both the animals and their human handlers is paramount. Your job involves building trust and a willing partnership as well as establishing firm leadership.

As a dog trainer, you will give private lessons or conduct classes that teach dogs to be good canine companions. You might specialize in certain types of training, such as working with service dogs that assist law enforcement or the disabled, training pet dogs, preparing pedigreed dogs for the show ring, or training working dogs. Most dog trainers work with pet dogs, and they must be as effective in training the owners as the dogs. As pets become more important members of their human families, demand for pet dog trainers is expected to rise.

It is not uncommon for avid equestrians to want to make their living working with the magnificent animals that they love so much, but it is rare for them to be successful. It would be disingenuous to pretend that horse training is not a difficult field to turn into a full time career, but it is certainly possible. The breadth of riding styles plus the sheer usefulness of horses gives you many points of entry into the horse world. Western riding and various forms of English riding, including hunt seat and dressage, remain popular around the country. Driving is enjoying a resurgence of interest, and thoroughbred racing remains a lucrative industry. The latest trend in horse training is natural horsemanship. A number of popular trainers are making a substantial living by teaching people how to obtain willing cooperation from their mounts without the use of fear or force. It is a great racket if you can cash in on it. If it does not appeal to you, rest assured that traditional training methods retain their popularity and you can hitch onto whatever style of training that suits you. Like all the careers covered in this volume, a few basic skills readily expanded can translate into a vocation that is challenging, rewarding, and above all appropriate to one's interest in the great outdoors.

Self-Assessment Quiz

I: Relevant Knowledge

1. How many years of specialized training have you had?
   - (a) None, it is not required
   - (b) Several weeks to several months of training
   - (c) A year-long course or other preparation
   - (d) Years of preparation in graduate or professional school, or equivalent job experience

2. Would you consider training to obtain certification or other required credentials?
   - (a) No
   - (b) Yes, but only if it is legally mandated
   - (c) Yes, but only if it is the industry standard
   - (d) Yes, if it is helpful (even if not mandatory)

3. In terms of achieving success, how would rate the following qualities in order from least to most important?
   - (a) ability, effort, preparation
   - (b) ability, preparation, effort
   - (c) preparation, ability, effort
   - (d) preparation, effort, ability

4. How would you feel about keeping track of current developments in your field?
   - (a) I prefer a field where very little changes
   - (b) If there were a trade publication, I would like to keep current with that
   - (c) I would be willing to regularly recertify my credentials or learn new systems
   - (d) I would be willing to aggressively keep myself up-to-date in a field that changes constantly

5. For whatever reason, you have to train a bright young successor to do your job. How quickly will he or she pick it up?
   (a) Very quickly
   (b) He or she can pick up the necessary skills on the job
   (c) With the necessary training he or she should succeed with hard work and concentration
   (d) There is going to be a long breaking-in period—there is no substitute for experience

II: Caring

1. How would you react to the following statement: "Other people are the most important thing in the world?"
   (a) No! Me first!
   (b) I do not really like other people, but I do make time for them
   (c) Yes, but you have to look out for yourself first
   (d) Yes, to such a degree that I often neglect my own well-being

2. Who of the following is the best role model?
   (a) Ayn Rand
   (b) Napoléon Bonaparte
   (c) Bill Gates
   (d) Florence Nightingale

3. How do you feel about pets?
   (a) I do not like animals at all
   (b) Dogs and cats and such are OK, but not for me
   (c) I have a pet, or I wish I did
   (d) I have several pets, and caring for them occupies significant amounts of my time

4. Which of the following sets of professions seems most appealing to you?
   (a) business leader, lawyer, entrepreneur
   (b) politician, police officer, athletic coach
   (c) teacher, religious leader, counselor
   (d) nurse, firefighter, paramedic

5. How well would you have to know someone to give them $100 in a harsh but not life-threatening circumstance? It would have to be...
   (a) ...a close family member or friend (brother or sister, best friend)
   (b) ...a more distant friend or relation (second cousin, coworkers)
   (c) ...an acquaintance (a coworker, someone from a community organization or church)
   (d) ...a complete stranger

III: Organizational Skills

1. Do you create sub-folders to further categorize the items in your "Pictures" and "Documents" folders on your computer?
   (a) No
   (b) Yes, but I do not use them consistently
   (c) Yes, and I use them consistently
   (d) Yes, and I also do so with my e-mail and music library

2. How do you keep track of your personal finances?
   (a) I do not, and I am never quite sure how much money is in my checking account
   (b) I do not really, but I always check my online banking to make sure I have money
   (c) I am generally very good about budgeting and keeping track of my expenses, but sometimes I make mistakes
   (d) I do things such as meticulously balance my checkbook, fill out Excel spreadsheets of my monthly expenses, and file my receipts

3. Do you systematically order commonly used items in your kitchen?
   (a) My kitchen is a mess
   (b) I can generally find things when I need them
   (c) A place for everything, and everything in its place
   (d) Yes, I rigorously order my kitchen and do things like alphabetize spices and herbal teas

4. How do you do your laundry?
   (a) I cram it in any old way
   (b) I separate whites and colors

(c) I separate whites and colors, plus whether it gets dried

(d) Not only do I separate whites and colors and drying or non-drying, I organize things by type of clothes or some other system

5. Can you work in clutter?
   (a) Yes, in fact I feel energized by the mess
   (b) A little clutter never hurt anyone
   (c) No, it drives me insane
   (d) Not only does my workspace need to be neat, so does that of everyone around me

IV: Communication Skills

1. Do people ask you to speak up, not mumble, or repeat yourself?
   (a) All the time
   (b) Often
   (c) Sometimes
   (d) Never

2. How do you feel about speaking in public?
   (a) It terrifies me
   (b) I can give a speech or presentation if I have to, but it is awkward
   (c) No problem!
   (d) I frequently give lectures and addresses, and I am very good at it

3. What's the difference between *their, they're,* and *there*?
   (a) I do not know
   (b) I know there is a difference, but I make mistakes in usage
   (c) I know the difference, but I can not articulate it
   (d) *Their* is the third-person possessive, *they're* is a contraction for *they are*, and *there is* a deictic adverb meaning "in that place"

4. Do you avoid writing long letters or e-mails because you are ashamed of your spelling, punctuation, and grammatical mistakes?
   (a) Yes
   (b) Yes, but I am either trying to improve or just do not care what people think

(c)   The few mistakes I make are easily overlooked

(d)   Save for the occasional typo, I do not ever make mistakes in usage

5.   Which choice best characterizes the most challenging book you are willing to read in your spare time?

(a)   I do not read

(b)   Light fiction reading such as the Harry Potter series, *The Da Vinci Code*, or mass-market paperbacks

(c)   Literary fiction or mass-market nonfiction such as history or biography

(d)   Long treatises on technical, academic, or scientific subjects

V: Mathematical Skills

1.   Do spreadsheets make you nervous?

(a)   Yes, and I do not use them at all

(b)   I can perform some simple tasks, but I feel that I should leave them to people who are better-qualified than myself

(c)   I feel that I am a better-than-average spreadsheet user

(d)   My job requires that I be very proficient with them

2.   What is the highest level math class you have ever taken?

(a)   I flunked high-school algebra

(b)   Trigonometry or pre-calculus

(c)   College calculus or statistics

(d)   Advanced college mathematics

3.   Would you rather make a presentation in words or using numbers and figures?

(a)   Definitely in words

(b)   In words, but I could throw in some simple figures and statistics if I had to

(c)   I could strike a balance between the two

(d)   Using numbers as much as possible; they are much more precise

4.   Cover the answers below with a sheet of paper, and then solve the following word problem: Mary has been legally able to vote for exactly half her life. Her husband John is three years older than she. Next year,

their son Harvey will be exactly one-quarter of John's age. How old was Mary when Harvey was born?
(a)   I couldn't work out the answer
(b)   25
(c)   26
(d)   27

5.   Cover the answers below with a sheet of paper, and then solve the following word problem: There are seven children on a school bus. Each child has seven book bags. Each bag has seven big cats in it. Each cat has seven kittens. How many legs are there on the bus?
(a)   I couldn't work out the answer
(b)   2,415
(c)   16,821
(d)   10,990

VI: Ability to Manage Stress

1.   It is the end of the working day, you have 20 minutes to finish an hour-long job, and you are scheduled to pick up your children. Your supervisor asks you why you are not finished. You:
(a)   Have a panic attack
(b)   Frantically redouble your efforts
(c)   Calmly tell her you need more time, make arrangements to have someone else pick up the kids, and work on the project past closing time
(d)   Calmly tell her that you need more time to do it right and that you have to leave, or ask if you can release this flawed version tonight

2.   When you are stressed, do you tend to:
(a)   Feel helpless, develop tightness in your chest, break out in cold sweats, or have other extreme, debilitating physiological symptoms?
(b)   Get irritable and develop a hair-trigger temper, drink too much, obsess over the problem, or exhibit other "normal" signs of stress?
(c)   Try to relax, keep your cool, and act as if there is no problem
(d)   Take deep, cleansing breaths and actively try to overcome the feelings of stress

3. The last time I was so angry or frazzled that I lost my composure was:
   (a) Last week or more recently
   (b) Last month
   (c) Over a year ago
   (d) So long ago I cannot remember

4. Which of the following describes you?
   (a) Stress is a major disruption in my life, people have spoken to me about my anger management issues, or I am on medication for my anxiety and stress
   (b) I get anxious and stressed out easily
   (c) Sometimes life can be a challenge, but you have to climb that mountain!
   (d) I am generally easygoing

5. What is your ideal vacation?
   (a) I do not take vacations; I feel my work life is too demanding
   (b) I would just like to be alone, with no one bothering me
   (c) I would like to do something not too demanding, like a cruise, with friends and family
   (d) I am an adventurer; I want to do exciting (or even dangerous) things and visit foreign lands

Scoring:

For each category...

For every answer of *a*, add zero points to your score.
For every answer of *b*, add ten points to your score.
For every answer of *c*, add fifteen points to your score.
For every answer of *d*, add twenty points to your score.

The result is your percentage in that category.

Forester

Forester

Career Compasses

Get your bearings on what it takes to be a successful forester.

Relevant Knowledge of environmental issues and threats to forest ecosystem health (40%)

Caring about forest preservation is an absolute necessity. You must really love trees, and the animals and plants that live in, under, and around them (30%)

Communication Skills to educate the public and deal with hikers, campers, hunters, and other recreational users of forests (20%)

Mathematical Skills are useful for measuring, tracking, mapping, surveying, and related tasks that are a regular part of the job of forester (10%)

Destination: Forester

If you are perusing this chapter because you are considering becoming a logger or lumberjack, keep reading to learn the differences between loggers and foresters. A forester may have occasion to fell trees, but only incidentally. That is not his or her main job. Foresters manage forests for human use. Forests are one type of terrestrial ecosystem that provide habitat for plant and animal species. Foresters can be involved in the conservation of these species and the restoration or preservation of the integrity of forest ecosystems. People sometimes want to preserve ecosystems or individual plant or animal species for aesthetic reasons, for moral reasons, or because these species aid humans in some way. Forests provide important protection for watersheds, which provide clean drinking water for human use. Forests also clean pollution out of the air and function as a carbon sink. Without healthy forests covering much of the surface of the Earth, humans could not survive. People use forests for recreation, hunting, and as a source of raw materials, including, but not limited to, timber. Foresters maintain forests for all of these varied uses. According to Gifford Pinochet, the first chief of the U.S. Forest Service and the founder of the Yale School of Forestry, the duty of a forester is to manage forest resources for "the greatest good for the greatest number in the long term." Perhaps because they are in tune with the slow growth of their tree charges, foresters take a long-term perspective, in contrast to the short-term perspective of most of the interests that compete for the use of forest resources.

Essential Gear

Take the road less traveled to physical fitness. Foresters walk a lot, and they spend time outdoors in rough terrain in all weather. Taking your exercise routine out of the gym and into the woods is great preparation for this line of work. Try trail running, mountain biking, biathlons and triathlons, canoeing, kayaking, mountain climbing, hiking, or whatever wilderness sports appeal to you. Any of these options is guaranteed to help your mind and body prepare for your new career.

Forestry is a profession and it is also a science. A bachelor's degree in forestry may be sufficient for some positions, but a master's degree is usually expected even for entry-level positions. While the median annual salary for foresters in 2006 was $51,900, this figure includes positions requiring an advanced degree. Foresters with a bachelor's degree can expect a starting salary of $28,000 to $36,000 per year; those entering the field with a master's can expect a starting salary in the range of $43,000 to $53,000per year. A job applicant with a doctorate can expect annual earnings of at least $63,000. Foresters employed by the federal government have higher earnings on average than those in the private sector, with a median salary of $65,964 in 2007. About two-thirds of foresters work for federal, state, or local governments. Job growth in forestry is not expected to be strong for the foreseeable future. There will be openings in both government and private sector forestry, but also look to conservation consulting as a potential area for employment.

Essential Gear

Pack your degree in your rucksack. Many of the jobs in this series on changing careers were chosen because you could transfer to them from another profession without too much difficulty. Forestry does have specific degree requirements, but they are not too onerous for the intrepid career changer. Start by going on an informational interview with someone in your target job and find out from them exactly what sort of degree and experience you need to get a similar job.

A major part of a forester's work is protecting forests from threats to their health. Diseases and insects can ravage trees. For example, urban foresters often find themselves dealing with Dutch elm disease, a fatal fungal disease that infects elm trees. There are also a variety of insects that can infest and devastate forests, against which foresters must remain vigilant.

Some foresters specialize exclusively in pest management. Of course, the main threat to forests these days is forest fires. Some wildfires are started by lightning strikes but the vast majority are started by humans. Foresters work to educate motorists, campers, and hikers on fire safety, and to spot arsonists who set fires deliberately. Most forest fires are first noted and reported by foresters on patrol, who coordinate and advise firefighters and other emergency personnel. Foresters often work alongside firefighters to put out forest fires, which makes forestry a physical and dangerous line of work.

Not all forest fires are bad, though. As part of the management of forested land, a forester will sometimes set a controlled burn. A controlled burn can minimize the chance of forest fires, as counterintuitive as it sounds. The uses planned for the land guide the decisions that a forester makes about burning, cutting trees, clearing brush, pulling or poisoning weeds, and allowing various species of seedlings to germinate or eradicating them.

The majority of foresters work in the area of procurement. Procurement foresters buy timber for companies that process it and sell it. They take inventories of trees on a given property, and decide what to cut when.

These foresters subcontract with loggers, cutters, and haulers, and they consult with crews on the building of roads to access the marked trees. Another important aspect of their job is making sure that they comply with environmental regulations, although the timber industry so dominates the regulatory process today that most regulations are weak or ignored without penalty.

Cutting trees is not the only way for landowners to generate income from forests. Hunting, fishing, and recreation can sometimes create a revenue stream. Once forested land has been logged, it is often not possible to replant trees there due to soil erosion, but newer logging techniques that avoid clear-cutting sometimes allow for replanting. Foresters choose where, when, and how formerly forested land will be replanted. This used to mean turning once diverse forests into tree farms with rows of identical trees, all the same age, just like a cornfield and just as unlike a real forest. But forestry techniques have improved, and tree farms are no longer the only option. The choices depend upon whether the landowner wants a quick profit or wants his foresters to manage his forest for long-term productivity and varied uses. Urban foresters' duties concern managing urban forests for recreation and for their aesthetic and healthful benefits to city dwellers, such as improvements in air quality, beautification, and urban wildlife habitat. Urban foresters also deal heavily with the effects of pollution on trees.

Although this fact might not strike you as obvious, forestry is a quickly evolving field. A significant percentage of foresters are employed in the area of research, and this is a particularly good option to consider if you have a background in the sciences, economics, or public policy. Research foresters work both in laboratories and in the field to conduct experiments and write articles and reports on innovative ways to improve forest health. Researchers look for ways to avoid soil erosion and improve soil and water quality. They search for methods of improving forest habitats for native species of wildlife, and restoring polluted and depleted forests. Some researchers focus exclusively on ways to increase the timber revenue of forests by researching less labor intensive and more efficient logging methods. The newest specialty within the profession of forestry is conservation. Conservation foresters focus on habitat protection rather than the more traditional emphasis on forest exploitation. These foresters also educate landowners and the public about forest stewardship.

You Are Here

You can begin your journey to becoming a forester from many different locales.

Do you work in a related field? There are a number of outdoor, scientific, or educational professions that could clear your path to a job as a forester. Farmers and ranchers are used to working outside on the land, which can help prepare you for this outdoor job. Environmental educators and conservationists are also well-placed to move into the field of forestry because they are familiar with ecosystem management issues and the specific threats that humans pose to forest health and preservation. Loggers, cutters, sawmill workers, and those in related timber processing jobs have some familiarity with the business side of forestry, but will need further education for this career change. So will wilderness firefighters, rescuers, and other emergency professionals who work regularly with foresters. Forestry is not a soft job and it is not for soft people, so do not expect a soft landing from wherever you enter.

Navigating the Terrain

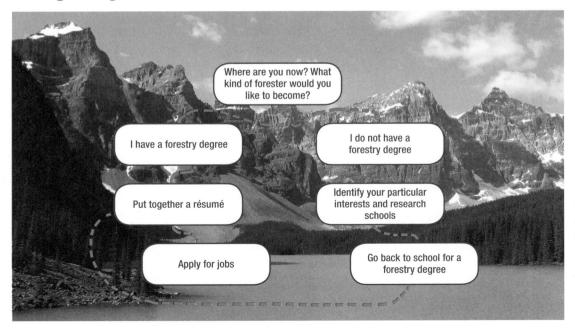

Do you have a forestry degree? For better or worse, getting a job as a forester requires a degree in forestry. A related degree or job experience might get you started in certain jobs, but you really need to obtain a degree in forestry to enter this field. This makes it a tough field for career changers because those entering it from another profession—even a closely related one such as conservation scientist—are unlikely to possess the requisite forestry degree. Keep this in mind as you contemplate your career change.

Are you in good physical condition? Foresters spend most of their workday outside, in all weather, far from the comforts of home. Foresters need to be tough and hardy. Forestry is not as dangerous a profession as logging, firefighting, or search and rescue, but foresters work closely with these occupations and take many of the same risks in the course of their duties.

Organizing Your Expedition

Before you set out, know where you are going.

Decide on a destination. What kind of forester would you like to be? Forestry is such a broad profession that you have the opportunity to specialize. The work of a forester employed by the government and one working in the private sector can be quite different. Foresters in public lands must manage them according to the guidelines of the U.S. Forest Service, which can, depending on the political winds, vacillate between a more conservation-oriented approach to a more resource-extractive attitude. Private sector foresters often advise landowners on how to manage their land to achieve their goals, whether those are conservation, habitat restoration, or resource extraction over various time periods. Specific areas of specialization that you could consider include: *wildlife management*, which includes culling species that are a nuisance, as well as species preservation, soil conservation, urban forestry, pest management, native species restoration, and removal of invasive flora and fauna; or *forest economics*, a field which looks at how to best exploit forest resources for human profit over a fixed time frame. Looking at available job openings in your area may help guide your choice of specialization, but let your interests, skills, and talents also play a role in helping you choose.

Notes from the Field

Laura Elizabeth Wooley
Urban forester
New York, New York

What were you doing before you decided to change careers?

I was working for a social service organization as a grant writer; however, most of the proposals I put together were not long shots. This was an organization with a large budget, a close relationship with city and state government, and a long track record.

Why did you change your career?

When I started working at this social service organization, I had just come to New York after having finished my second of two years in China. I was fluent in Chinese, had no idea what I wanted to do, and had made the rash decision to come to New York without any job prospects. I quickly grew bored and began working on ways to get out of my situation, and that's how I started looking at graduate programs. I had the idea in mind that I needed to get at least a master's degree. But beyond that, of course, I felt that I had a lot of intellectual exploration to do.

How did you make the transition?

Since I wasn't totally clear on anything except that I needed to get out of my current situation, I actually applied to two programs in landscape architecture (which I now know I would have hated), but ended up choosing to attend Yale School of Forestry & Environmental Studies. Before starting the program, I had the idea that I would be a school science teacher specializing in environmental education, but while in school I tried on several different careers for a bit (including environmental journalist and urban/community forester). The work I did as a community forestry intern in New Haven was the best fit for me, and it's what connected me to my current employer here in New York City. In New Haven, I enjoyed the face-to-face interaction and collaboration with community

Scout the terrain. Your first step on the path to your new career may involve returning to school for a forestry degree. To that end, investigate what schools in your area offer programs in forestry. If no program

members in the planning and implementation of real projects with real results—such as tree planting, the creation of small community gardens, etc. I was hired by my current employer partly because I had developed strong skills in interacting with the community, and upon arrival became responsible for a tree donation program as well as a tree care training program. Now I am implementing a project that combines street tree planting with community outreach and education.

What are the keys to success in your new career?

Working as an urban forester takes an ability to listen to people's concerns and come up with whatever solutions are workable from an institutional point of view. It also takes a certain clearheadedness about what your responsibilities are to individual community members. You're talking to people about the components of their local infrastructure; trees are a part of that picture, and they happen to interact physically with utility lines, sidewalks, buildings, cars, and so on. When you're talking to someone about trees, you are opening up a can of worms because you may open up some longstanding grievances about perceived government neglect of the infrastructural components of their block or neighborhood, i.e., "This stop sign post has been bent and leaning into the street for 3 years now and nobody has come to fix it—I called 311 two years ago and nothing was ever done." What an urban forester does is different depending on where you work and the entity for which you work. What we foresters in New York City Parks & Recreation do is quite different from what someone would be doing in a much smaller city. Working for the City of New York, you must always be aware of the colossus that is the city bureaucracy. In smaller cities and organizations, there is a lot more tree planting done by hand with community involvement, whereas we are hiring large landscaping contractors to do the planting, seeking or agreeing to very little coordination with the community. Someone who has requested a tree will wait and wait and then wake up one morning to a jackhammer breaking up their sidewalk to make room for a tree.

works, consider whether you are willing to move to attend school. If you have a forestry degree already, then this stage of the game will involve looking at available jobs in your area. In most areas with substantial forest cover, some of the land is likely to be in private hands, and some publicly owned. Consider whether you live in an urban or rural area, and what interests dominate economically. If you are interested in research, look for large research universities with schools of forestry nearby. If the available options do not interest you, contemplate a move to an area that offers the type of forestry job you desire.

Find the path that's right for you. If your current job is far from the realm of forestry, give some thought not just to the specific job you think you want but to the kind of lifestyle you desire. The job opportunities within forestry are surprisingly diverse. If you want to get out of your cubicle but you do not want to be far from the city, jobs in urban forestry, research, public policy, and education can keep you within sight of the skyscrapers. If, on the contrary, you are drawn to forestry because you prefer the company of trees to humans, there are plenty of jobs that will allow you to spend most of your time alone in the forest.

Go back to school. Check the Society of American Foresters Web site for a list of 50 schools with accredited forestry programs leading to a first professional degree in forestry (bachelor's or master's level). Forestry is offered as a major at a number of public and private schools across the country, including prestigious universities, such as Yale. But whether you go to an Ivy League institution or attend a community college, there is a packing list of variables that you must consider before you embark. Look first at the curriculum. Does it offer the courses you need to proceed from your current background into a viable forestry career? Consider also the size of the institution. Does its size suit you, based upon your self-knowledge and previous education? Some people thrive in a large public university environment, with its many resources. Others will sacrifice variety of resources for the intimacy and attention of small classes. Where is the school located? Can you commute there easily or would you have to move? Can you attend school part time whilst you maintain your current employment, or would you have to attend full time? In either case, what are the costs of attendance, such as tuition and fees and textbooks and supplies? Is there financial aid available? Check your eligibility for scholarships, grants and student loans at schools that interest you. Last but not least, look at the job placement record of the institution. Are their degrees and/or certifications respected by employers? Are they successful in placing their graduates? Do they have a career office that assists students in their search for employment in forestry? The answers to these questions will help you choose the right school for your needs, preferences, financial situation, and career aspirations.

Landmarks

If you are in your twenties . . . If you have decided that you want to become a forester, the first step is to get a forestry degree. If you are an undergraduate, find out if your current institution offers a forestry major. Transfer to a school that offers it as a major if you must. If that is not feasible or desirable for you, major in environmental sciences, natural resources management, or biology, any of which can help you get started in forestry. If you are not currently in school, apply for forestry programs.

If you are in your thirties or forties . . . You will need to begin your career change by getting a forestry degree, so your first task will be applying to schools that offer a forestry major. If you are near a forestry school, and work in a related field, such as environmental sciences, you may be able to arrange to return to school part time and maintain your current employment, possibly adjusting your hours to accommodate your class schedule.

If you are in your fifties . . . If you are contemplating a career in forestry, you should have work experience in a closely related and transferable field, or the ability to return to school full time for a forestry degree.

If you are over sixty . . . Consider the advice for fifties career changers applicable to you, and also work on building, if necessary, and maintaining your fitness for this physically challenging profession. Any closely related and transferable work experience will look good on your résumé. You are unlikely to encounter age-related job discrimination in this field, but be vigilant for it anyway.

Further Resources

Society of American Foresters This is the main professional membership organization for foresters. It is well-established throughout the country, having existed since 1900. Its Web site provides lots of information about education and certification for forestry, among other resources. http://www.safnet.org

U.S. Forest Service The Web site of the federal government department. Site includes employment information. http://www.fs.fed.us

Sustainable Forests Partnership An organization formed at the University of Oregon to promote innovate sustainable forestry practices. Site includes many useful links. http://sfp.cas.psu.edu

Forest Stewardship Council (United States) A worldwide coalition of normally antagonistic stakeholders in the forestry sector that promotes responsible forest management and certifies wood products as harvested in a sustainable way. http://www.fscus.org

Organic Farmer

Organic Farmer

Career Compasses

Get your bearings on what it takes to be a successful organic farmer.

Relevant Knowledge of growing crops and raising livestock (40%)

Caring about the environment and historic preservation is an absolute necessity for a small farmer (30%)

Mathematical Skills to accurately do your farm accounting and bookkeeping (20%)

Ability to Manage Stress is crucial because farming is risky business, both financially and physically (10%)

Destination: Organic Farmer

So green acres is the place you want to be? The appeal of farming in the modern world is easy to understand. In contrast to urbanites who toil in hermetically-sealed office towers under florescent lights, often unaware if it is night or day and stressed by artificial deadlines and over-scheduled lives, farmers seem in touch with the rhythms of nature, enjoying a slower pace of life and smelling trees and flowers instead of car exhaust.

They hear crickets instead of car horns, the crackle of a fireplace instead of the inane chatter of an overcrowded bar. Farmers rise with the sun and go to bed early. They are in tune with the seasons and with the cycle of life. Their lifestyle seems old-fashioned and evokes nostalgia for simpler times. In a society of mass-produced, over-processed, and imported goods, farmers are our link to the origins of things. Ultimately, that processed red blob of chemicals on your McDonald's fries started life as a tomato ripening under the warm sun on a farm, and even those fries—hard as it is to believe in their highly processed state—started out as potatoes that had to be dug from the cool, damp earth.

Of course, fast food chains don't get their produce from small farms; they purchase it from the gigantic agribusinesses that have made small family farmers a dying breed. The consolidation of farms into giant conglomerates has reduced the number of farms in the country significantly. By producing large amounts of food more cheaply and efficiently, it has not been easy for family farms to stay in business. Many farmers have sold out and their children have moved away from rural life. But all is not lost quite yet. The growth of the organic food movement and the more recent Slow Food and "localvore" movements have given small farmers a new niche to fill. The local market is a new playing field that does not give complete advantage to giant agribusinesses. Look around at the non-chain restaurants in your area and see how many of them boast that they obtain their eggs or meat or produce locally and, in many cases, organically. Shops that cater to tourists, as well as bakeries, farm stands, kiosks, and coffee houses often feature local baked goods and preserves. Even supermarket chains like Whole Foods have local produce that is clearly and proudly labeled as such. As environmental consciousness grows along with the cost of fuel, the market for locally produced food and related farm products is only going to grow. This creates an opportunity for small farmers that has not existed in this country since the eighteenth and nineteenth centuries.

The current credit and real estate markets do not make it easy to obtain a mortgage, but if you can afford it there are plenty of farms for sale or rent. Many are available due to the retirement of older farmers. Sometimes these former owners make themselves available to help new farmers learn the business. Some farmers are even willing to rent out their farms instead of selling them outright, to help a nascent farmer get started. Organizations like New England's Land Link (NELL) are useful for finding out about opportunities to help you ease the transition into owning your own farm. Getting a farm is only the first step in becoming a real, live farmer. If you do not have a background in farming, the challenges involved in cultivating even a small piece of land or raising even a small number of livestock can be daunting. Having an intrepid thirst for new knowledge and the ability and willingness to do a lot of research are crucial prerequisites to exchanging your cubicle for a John Deere. But having the advice of an experienced farmer is invaluable.

If you are contemplating becoming a farmer at all, you are probably asking yourself if you should farm organically. The answer, in a word, is yes. Organic is the way of the future, just as it was the way of the past, before the advent of agrochemicals. Agrochemicals increased the yield of crops by providing them with resistance to pests, but we have learned that this comes at a high cost to human and animal health and the environment. Consumers are increasingly demanding produce that has been grown without the aid of agrochemicals and farmers have been responding by phasing out their use. Chemicals, not just for crops but for livestock too, helped to make farming less labor intensive and promoted the growth of huge factory farms. A return to organic pest

Essential Gear

Get third-party organic certified. In order to legally label and market your farm produce as "organic," you need to obtain official certification. There used to be many different certification schemes in the United States, each with its own definition of "organic." With the passage of the Organic Food Production Act in 1990 and the subsequent implementation of the National Organic Program Regulations in 2001, there are now uniform national standards that must be followed by all third-party certification agencies. Once you pick an agency, you will have to supply them with detailed information about your farm operations, as well as maps of your farm. An organic inspector will then come out to look at your farm and submit a report to the certification committee. After the committee's review, you may get the certification you desire, or it may be denied. A common reason for denial is a lack of adequate records, so be sure yours are sufficient by finding out now what you will need to track in order to receive organic certification. If you are meticulous and keep working towards your goal, you will eventually be able to call yourself a certified organic farmer.

management creates new opportunities for the small-scale, hands-on farmer to get back in the game and dovetails nicely with the locally grown movement.

The growing concern with where our food comes from and what is in it has extended to animal products as well as produce. Here the issues extend beyond human health and the environment to moral concerns about how animals raised for food are treated. Concern for animal welfare has led to consumers choosing eggs from cage-free hens and beef from cattle grass fed on pastures instead of cooped up in feedlots. Most states are passing legislation regulating the conditions under which farm animals can be kept, increasingly giving small farmers an opportunity to compete with factory farms for market share.

If you have read this far, you are probably full of questions, ideas, and enthusiasm for your career change into farming. There is a lot that you need to learn to become a successful small farmer, and a lot of decisions you will need to make wisely to get your new business up and running. This chapter provides a basic overview of the small farm business for the novice and provides links to other sources of information. Farmers need to make money, of course, and it is dangerous to forget it is a business, but farmers also end their work day with a sense of accomplishment that can only come from seeing the fruits of their own physical labor. As a profession it is a fitting antidote to the modern world. It used to be said that you could not keep people down on the farm once they had seen the big city. Now it seems we cannot get back to the farm fast enough.

You Are Here

You can begin your journey to organic farming from many different locales.

Did you grow up on a farm? This is useful for two reasons. The first reason is that farming is hard work. If you have not grown up on a farm or studied agricultural science in school, you may not fully grasp the backbreaking tedium and hazards of farmwork. You may be in danger of romanticizing the idea of making your living off the land, not realizing that means being out on the land in all weather. The second reason that related experience is helpful is because farming requires specialized knowledge. You need to know a vast amount about crops, soil, irrigation, livestock, equipment, and the latest developments in farming technology, as well as other skills that are best acquired through experience.

Essential Gear

Find one thing that makes you outstanding in your field. The recent national emphasis on buying locally grown food combined with the organic and back-to-the land movements have led to a proliferation of farmers' markets and restaurants, delis, bakeries, gourmet shops and other food outlets advertising that they sell locally grown food. While this creates more opportunities for you, it also creates more competition. Why should local businesses stock your eggs or butternut squash when there are ten other local farms offering the same products? The key to success is not simply underpricing your competitors; you need to find a way to make your farm products stand out. This can include a catchy name, unusual combinations of ingredients, finding unusual and heirloom varieties of produce, or offering a little something extra, like a booklet of apple recipes with each bushel sold. The possibilities are endless, so make like a hen and get brooding on what makes your farm special and unique.

Do you have an agriculture-related degree? Do you know how to measure soil pH and how to assist a birthing ewe? Although farming may seem to be a low-tech, labor-intensive industry, it is a science. Every decision you make for your crops about seeds, fertilizer, pest management, irrigation, and equipment, and every decision you make for your animals regarding food, breeding, living conditions, veterinary care, and vaccinations, has to be based on knowledge that you have acquired somewhere. Even farmers who were raised on farms go to college to study the agricultural sciences so they can more effectively and efficiently manage their farms.

Do you have another source of income? If you have ever planted a seed or bred an animal, you may have noticed that there is a bit of a time delay between germination or conception and the maturity of your fruit, vegetable, or animal. Not only does it take time to get your produce to market, but there are many things that can go wrong which will prevent it from getting there at all. Weather and pests can conspire against your harvest and, sadly, animals can become ill or injured. The safest way to enter farming is to start with it as a hobby and not count on your farm as a reliable source of income.

Navigating the Terrain

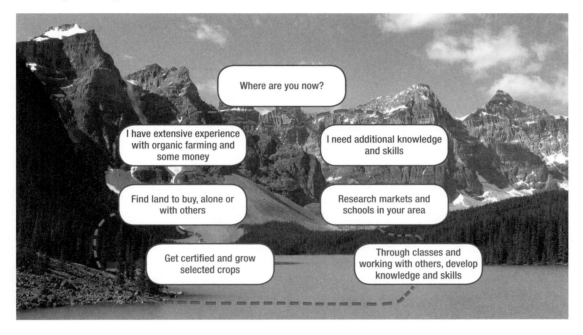

Where are you now?

I have extensive experience with organic farming and some money

I need additional knowledge and skills

Find land to buy, alone or with others

Research markets and schools in your area

Get certified and grow selected crops

Through classes and working with others, develop knowledge and skills

Organizing your Expedition

Before you set out, know where you are going.

Decide on a destination. What kind of organic farmer would you like to be? Some farmers grow fruits and vegetables, which they sell in a raw, unprocessed state. Other farmers raise domesticated livestock, such as poultry, cattle, pigs, goats, and sheep. In some cases, the animals themselves are sold for meat; in other cases, the farmer sells the eggs, milk, fleece, or other products produced by live animals. Not all farm products are unprocessed. Some farmers sell ice cream, cheese, butter, buttermilk, sour cream, and other dairy products made from their cows', goats', or sheep's milk. Some sell roving or yarn spun and dyed from sheep, llama, alpaca, or angora rabbit fleece. A considerable number of farmers make jams, jellies, and other preserves from their fruits. Some even sell baked goods, and quite a few farms offer pick-your-own fruit opportunities for customers when berries, apples, pumpkins, and other

Notes from the Field

Sarah Williams
Apprentice farmer
Ghent, New York

What were you doing before you decided to change careers?

I transitioned to farming from a career in nonprofit advocacy. I was working for an organization called the Drug Policy Alliance doing drug policy reform. Our work included a harm-reduction education model for young people, medical marijuana legislation, treatment instead of incarceration legislation, needle-exchange legislation, and research and media work. It was very good work, striving towards drug policies based on reason, compassion and justice, but I was unsatisfied in the big city, with the hassles of commuting, office politics, etc.

Why did you change your career?

As I mentioned, I got very unhappy working in Manhattan; there was especially something about commuting that I knew I could not tolerate indefinitely. I longed for community, working where I lived, and doing something less abstract, and more grounding. I also always felt drawn to physical work but, having been trained by a traditional education system, those sorts of jobs were never on the top of the typical career list.

How did you make the transition?

I transitioned very smoothly through an apprenticeship program. A lot of small organic farms are turning to apprentices these days because

popular hand-picking crops are ripe. Your farm can have both animals and crops, or just one or the other. It is up to you, and you can always start small and add more crops or livestock later.

Scout the terrain. Your farming options will depend upon the region where your farm is located. You are not likely to start a successful orange grove in Vermont or be able to grow cranberries in Arizona. Climate, sun, soil, and terrain are all important characteristics to consider in deciding what plants or animals will thrive in your local environment. If you do *they are affordable labor and because farmers genuinely want to encourage people to enter this field and galvanize the movement. The apprenticeship was great. I lived with three other people age 25-30; our housing and utilities were included and we had access to everything the farm produced, which in my case included veggies, raw milk, yogurt, a variety of hard and soft chesses, bakery goods, and sauerkraut. We were also paid a fair salary that was easy to live on. Most apprentices stay in that position (at various farms) for a few years, although you could ostensibly get a manager's job or start your own place with less experience.*

What are the keys to success in your new career?

The keys to success are tapping into the network of available mentors and resources. It is amazing how many people, organizations, and Web sites you can connect with that can help you in various ways to start your career or your own small farm. It is really a grassroots, community-based movement and once you take your first step (i.e., an apprenticeship) the opportunities really open themselves to you. But as far as advice is concerned—the season is not a race, it is a marathon, and keeping a positive outlook, your body well stretched, and a good group of people to bounce ideas (or frustrations) off of is really all a person needs to farm. The rest comes pretty naturally with experience.

not already own a farm, consider what crops or animals you would like to raise before you decide where to purchase land. If you have inherited a farm or do not have a choice about location for other reasons, start by going to local farmers' markets in various seasons and assessing what is grown locally. Talk to local farmers and find out what crops work best for the climate and soil in your area. Consider what outlets exist to sell small farm produce in your region, and find out what is selling well in these venues. Visit county and state fairs and other agricultural shows to meet farmers in your area and ask questions.

Find the path that's right for you. As you contemplate your career change from cubicle denizen to organic farmer, the choices and the amount of specific knowledge needed to pursue any of them may seem overwhelming. In that case, the most sensible approach is to start small. If you want to raise sheep, do not run out and buy 100 of them tomorrow. Start with a pair and take your time learning what is necessary to keep them healthy and happy. If, on the other hand, you are already feeling confident, still take the time to make a business plan. Consider how much you have to invest in starting your organic farm and how much money you will need to make from it. Show your plan to an agricultural manager to get a sense of how realistic it is. Then roll up your sleeves and get started living your farm dream!

Go back to school. As a self-employed farmer, you are not looking for a degree to put on your résumé to attract potential employers, but the variety of knowledge that you need to be a successful farmer can be acquired in an agricultural sciences program. Most state universities started out as agricultural colleges, so they are the first place to look for potential programs. Every state university system contains at least one agricultural college that will offer classes in horticulture, crop and fruit science, agronomy, dairy science, the environmental impact of agrochemicals, and animal husbandry. You will need to learn both the science and the business sides of farming, so look for courses in agricultural economics and farm management. Seek out opportunities for apprenticeships that will enable you to learn how to apply what you are learning in the classroom to real life situations with variable weather and soil conditions. Farming is not a profession where book learning is enough; it is a necessary but not sufficient condition for success.

Landmarks

If you are in your twenties . . . A lot will depend upon your background. If you were a 4-Her who grew up on a farm, then your main challenge is going to be affording your own farm at such a young age. If you cannot get a mortgage yet, consider working as a farm manager or going back to school to get a degree in agricultural sciences.

If you are in your thirties or forties . . . If you own or have access to land, you might find that you can grow and sell produce as a sideline occupation at first. If you are able to quit your current job and take the plunge into organic farming full time, you can look into getting an internship or leasing a farm from a retiring farmer who might show you the ropes.

If you are in your fifties . . . If you spent your career in another field than the kind that is filled with rows of crops, even if you grew up on a farm, you are going to have to get some education in current farming techniques and the laws governing organic certification, farm income taxes, and related issues. You do not necessarily need to go back to school for a formal degree since you are looking to be self-employed, but you will need to read and educate yourself before hitching your wagon to your new profession.

If you are over sixty . . . Then you may have the advantage of retirement income that will let you transition slowly into organic farming without depending upon it as your sole means of support. This is a great time of life to take up farming, as long as you are hale enough to handle the rigorous outdoor labor of farm life.

Further Resources

National FFA Organization   This site provides information about education and jobs in the agricultural sciences. http://www.ffa.org
U.S. Department of Agriculture   The USDA Web site provides general information about agricultural developments, regulations and employment. http://www.usda.gov/wps/portal/usdahome
Local Harvest   This national list of farms that sell sustainably grown, mainly organic products. Get your farm registered with them when you are ready to sell your products.   http://www.localharvest.org
Organic Farming Research Foundation   This organization sponsors research and education to promote the adoption of organic farming practices. They have grants available for farmers. http://ofrf.org/index.html

Rancher

Rancher

Career Compasses

Get your bearings on what it takes to be a successful rancher.

Relevant Knowledge of livestock and rangeland management (60%)

Caring about the local wildlife is important, because ranchers are often in conflict with wild predators (20%)

Mathematical Skills to accurately do your ranch accounting and bookkeeping (10%)

Ability to Manage Stress is crucial because ranching is a perilous business, both financially and physically (10%)

Destination: Rancher

If you have got a hankering to find a new home on the range, you have come to the right place. This chapter will round up some of the information you need to corral your ranching ambitions and turn your dream into a day-to-day lifestyle reality. Ranching is considered not so much a career as a vocation—an intensely masculine, testosterone-laden occupation—with a history wrapped up in the romanticism of the Old West. The ranch gave us the cowboy, symbol of a man who is his own boss, solitary on his long rides, and tough enough to handle the harsh weather of the plains and hills, the snake bites, and the nasty work of castrating and branding animals. In American political culture, the West connotes self-sufficiency and freedom from government interference (although, ironically, government land grants and hefty subsidies are necessary for their very existence today). On the frontier, you were alone to defend yourself, your family, and your property. Everyone in the family had to pitch in to survive, and the hired help consisted of cowboys who were men little in need of human warmth and companionship. The myth of the American West, just like the more general myth of the American dream, is alive and well in American culture today. It may be this romanticization of the rigors of ranch life that compels you to read this chapter. After a long day at your desk in the oppressive atmosphere of an office building, you may long for the rocking motion of a horse's lope, the creak of a saddle, and a view of the sunset that is not on your computer's desktop background.

Essential Gear

Sharp business skills will brand you as a winner. Ranching has many romantic connotations but do not forget for a minute that it is business. Ranchers raise livestock to sell at a profit. Every decision made on a ranch involves a careful cost-benefit analysis. You will face many choices as the price of meat fluctuates on domestic and international markets. What type of livestock should you raise and the money you spend to check on them on the range, vaccinate them, and otherwise care for them involves precise calculations of what you need to do to make a profit. A rancher cannot get away with just having a talent for roping calves or rounding up steer. He or she needs to be a skillful business manager with a head for figures as well as horses.

To start with, there are several different types of ranches. Working ranches generate most of their income from livestock that are raised for their meat. Working ranches are usually very large in terms of acreage and very modest in terms of modern amenities. They are the closest to the Old West idea of scratching out a rough living from the land. Some ranches may have crops as well as livestock. The animals raised are most often cattle, sold for beef, but bison and sheep are not uncommon. A few ranches raise more exotic animals, including stock for hunting. A large, well-off ranch may employ many ranch hands, sometimes seasonally, and provide bunkhouses or other accommodation for them on the property. The house may be well-appointed with many modern amenities, but a working ranch is the more likely to be rustic and isolated.

Another type of ranch is the dude ranch. A dude rancher earns his or her income from tourists who come to horseback ride at the ranch. Most dude ranches offer a variety of rural attractions, such as hay and sleigh rides, cross-country skiing, fishing, hunting, hiking, and campfires with traditional "cowboy" food and games. Dude ranches usually have rustic accommodations for guests, sometimes in log buildings. Running a dude ranch requires a background not only in the activities you offer, but in the hospitality industry. Dude ranches are popular vacation destinations for Americans. They often inspire visitors to want their own ranch.

The next type of ranch is the recreational ranch. This ranch type is usually medium to large in size and beautifully situated. Like a dude ranch, its income derives from vacationers seeking fresh air and outdoor exercise such as hunting or fishing, but it tends to be a bit more upscale with a focus on the location rather than activities such as horseback riding. A small recreational ranch is sometimes called a gentleman's ranch. This ranch may offer the amenities of a recreational ranch, but only be open only to the owner's family and friends and supported by his or her outside wealth. A small ranch with ample upscale amenities such as golf, tennis, swimming, and fine dining, and which may be fenced for privacy, is known as a resort ranch. As with a dude ranch, a prospective owner of a resort ranch should have extensive experience in the higher end of the hospitality industry.

Finally, an estate ranch is really a glorified suburban house, with some open land nearby and room for a horse or two. This chapter will focus on building you a roadmap to ownership of a working ranch, although we will also consider the possibility that you are looking to open some type of guest ranch and provide some assistance toward that goal.

The small, family owned working ranch is not seeing quite the revival experienced recently by the small family farm. As most ranching moves into the hands of giant agribusiness conglomerates, many more people are leaving ranching than entering it. Most ranch hands work for these conglomerates rather than for themselves. But the local and organic movements that are making small family farms viable again have not completely bypassed ranchers. There is a desire among consumers for meat that is not imported from South American countries like Argentina or Brazil, and for assurances that animals were raised without the use of hormones, antibiotics, and unnatural feeds. Grass-fed or range-raised beef is more desirable than beef from cattle stuck in feedlots. Organic beef commands a high price in the American market today, as does more exotic meat like bison—which is becoming so common that a bison burger can hardly be called unusual anymore. Raising animals organically is more labor-intensive and harder to do on a large scale. Thus family ranchers can enter a market that agribusiness conglomerates have come to dominate. If you are considering buying a working ranch, it is pretty much essential that you make a commitment to raising grass-fed, organic meat. Not only is this better morally and environmentally, but it is the only way you can compete with the big companies.

You Are Here

You can begin your journey to ranching from many different locales.

Do you work in a related field? In frontier days, a novice rancher could starve to death or worse. He could fall victim to the same predators that killed his livestock, or find that his meal ticket had wandered off the mountainside and was nowhere to be found at round-up time. Today the risks are more financial than physical, although many threats to life and limb abound on ranches. The more you know before you start, the less likely you are to wind up with dead livestock, a dry well, or an empty bank account. If you have worked in any capacity in agriculture, especially with farm animals, you have an advantage over someone whose rear end has never warmed a saddle before. Business experience is just as useful, especially if you can hire people to assist and advise you.

Can you ride Western? It is true that most cowboys ride in trucks today. In the same way that crop-growing family farms are swallowed by huge conglomerates, so goes the family ranch. The resulting size of these modern agribusiness super-ranches makes it impractical to manage livestock on horseback the old-fashioned way. Nonetheless, horseback riding remains a traditional part of ranch life. Some small family ranchers generate most of their income from operating a dude ranch where city slickers come to get a taste of the cowboy lifestyle. Leading group rides and giving basic lessons and demonstrations in Western horsemanship, herding and roping cattle, and related equine activities is expected of you as a rancher.

Navigating the Terrain

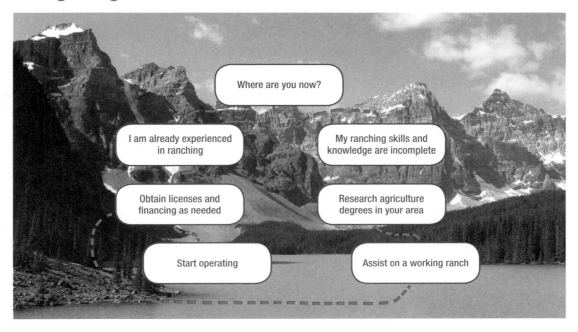

Where are you now?

I am already experienced in ranching

My ranching skills and knowledge are incomplete

Obtain licenses and financing as needed

Research agriculture degrees in your area

Start operating

Assist on a working ranch

Are you an avid outdoor sportsman? It is rare today for a rancher to earn all of his or her income from marketing livestock for meat. Many ranchers open up their land to recreational sportsman, offering various amenities from basic camping to a luxury resort. Leading hunting and fishing expeditions and knowing the exact fish and waterfowl to be found on your property are invaluable skills for attracting additional income from visiting hunters.

Organizing your Expedition

Before you set out, know where you are going.

Decide on a destination. Changing your career opens up the kind of broad horizons that we associate with the American West. Whilst the choices you face as you ride off into the sunset of your new career are not as limitless as the prairie horizon, they can seem that way. Ranching is

Notes from the Field

Jeremiah Johnson
Cattle rancher
Austin, Texas

What were you doing before you decided to change careers?

Well, I did a few things. I majored in economics at the University of Texas, and my first job out of school was as a bank teller. I left that job to become a commodities trader. I traded futures on the Chicago Mercantile Exchange until leaving to become a venture capitalist. Then I semi-retired from that and bought my ranch.

Why did you change your career?

I felt I had taken advantage of the opportunities life had given me and I felt ready to return to my roots in Texas.

a fairly varied field insofar as ranchers raise different types of livestock; feed, care for, and enclose that livestock differently; and have different supplemental businesses to make ends meet.

Scout the terrain. There are ten Western states in particular that are associated with ranching: Arizona, California, Colorado, Idaho, Montana, New Mexico, Oregon, Utah, Washington, and Wyoming. There are also ranches in some nearby states, such as the Dakotas. Consider first where you want to live, then the type of ranching you want to undertake. Some ranchers graze their animals on their own property. Others have grazing rights on public lands. Many ranchers earn a portion of their income from allowing hunting and/or fishing on their land. If that is in your plans, you need to assess the availability of lakes, rivers, and streams, the local wildlife types, and the hunting laws in that area. If you are opening a dude ranch, consider how accessible the location is for tourists traveling from far away. Thinking of opening a resort ranch? You will need to assess the local amenities. If you are buying a property that is already set up as a resort, you may have to compromise on location to get the best property. If you plan on renovating a ranch to add the appropriate amenities to turn it into a dude, resort, or any kind of guest ranch,

How did you make the transition?

I had inherited my parents' house in Austin, but I never lived in it. When I decided to return to Texas, I sold my house in Highland Park (a suburb of Chicago) and bought a 450-acre working cattle ranch outside Austin. I still have my parents' house. Don't know what I will do with that.

What are the keys to success in your new career?

Don't pretend to know more than you do. Down here everyone has a Texas size ego, so it's hard to ask for help or admit you don't know something. I enjoy my ranch, and I run it as a business, but I rely on my staff to handle the day-to-day operations.

make sure that you check out zoning restrictions and local construction costs before committing to a particular property.

Find the path that's right for you. Taking up ranching is different from becoming a farmer in that the start-up costs are higher and the learning curve steeper. It is easier to grow a few vegetables and work your way up to making a living at farming than it is to graze a few head of cattle. Ranching and farming are both labor-intensive, but, like the vast Western ranges where it was born, ranching does everything on a grand scale. The fact that it is hard to start small makes the leap into ranching a big one. One way to ease the transition (if you can afford it) is to buy a ranch as a second property that you use first for vacationing and hunting. You can get your feet wet (or dusty, as the case may be) over several years as you gradually spend more time there, bringing in livestock and employees to manage your new venture. Few people who go into ranching today do so expecting it to be their sole source of income. On the contrary, they tend to be wealthy individuals who buy a gentleman's ranch as their personal playground and later discover that there is a market for renting it to hunters or that they can easily make a profit from letting cattle graze on their land.

Go back to school. You do not need a fancy degree to ride a fence line or rope a steer. Most of what you need to know to be a successful rancher can only be learned by doing. But there are a few exceptions: Both the animal husbandry and business ends of ranching certainly involve skills that must be honed on the job, but you can get a leg up by studying them in school. An undergraduate degree in business with a concentration in agricultural business is one option. Ensure that the program contains courses in agricultural economics. A degree in agricultural science with a concentration in animal husbandry, pre-veterinary, livestock, or farm management would also be useful. There are not many degrees in ranching per se, but when you are looking at schools, bear in mind that every state has a public agricultural college and the ones in traditional Western ranching states are most likely to offer courses that are specific to ranching in particular. If you are looking for a master's degree, Texas A&M–Kingville's Institute for Ranch Management offers the first-ever graduate-level degree for ranchers. It is an exclusive two-year program with courses ranging from wildlife and rangeland management to market analysis using advanced math.

Essential Gear

A passion for hard work is your passport to success. Ranching is hard, physical outdoor labor punctuated by long hours of bookkeeping and gnarly personnel management issues. Ranchers do not get paid vacation days nor does work cease on major holidays. Ranching does not come with a retirement plan, health insurance or other benefits. If a good 401(k) and dental/vision coverage are priorities for you in a job search, ranching may not be right for you. If your ranch becomes profitable, you may be able to hire enough help that you can take a day off once in awhile, but do not count on that, at least in the short-term. Plan on working long hours, seven days a week, and putting your heart and soul into making your ranch a profitable business as well as a labor of love.

Landmarks

If you are in your twenties . . . You should consider getting a job as a ranch hand. As noted above, taking agricultural economics and farm/ranch business management courses is a good idea, but so is getting some first-hand experience. Working on a ranch is the best way to determine if being a rancher is the career for you.

If you are in your thirties or forties . . . If you are considering leaving your current job to become a rancher, you need to have a sound business plan and a way to pay for your ranch and survive financially until you turn a profit. Basically, you need to think through the financial end of your career change before you dismount from your current career.

If you are in your fifties . . . The first concern that comes to mind is money. As a neophyte rancher, you are unlikely to see a profit for some years. Make sure that you can afford health benefits and that you will not have to dip into your retirement savings to start your new ranching business or keep it afloat. If you haven't been self-employed so far in your career, consider taking some business courses before you buy a ranch of your own.

If you are over sixty . . . The question of why you are considering segueing into such a hard life is inevitable. Certainly people are remaining healthy and fit longer each year, and many retirees are seeking challenging new careers and taking on new physical and mental challenges. But the life of a rancher is quite harsh. If you want to take it on, more power to you, but do consider its physical demands realistically before you commit to this career change.

Further Resources

Beginning Farmer and Rancher Resources This site provides information on bookkeeping, taxes and other financial matters. It is written by an accountant. http://beginingfarmerrancher.wordpress.com

Center for Rural Affairs A "nationally recognized policy analysis and advocacy organization focused on the upper Midwest and Great Plains" that advocates for policies that benefit farmers and ranchers, promote sustainable agriculture and help beginning farmers and ranchers. http://www.cfra.org

National Sustainable Agriculture Information Service A government-sponsored organization that provides information and technical assistance to farmers and ranchers. http://www.attra.ncat.org

Land Trust Alliance This site provides leadership and expertise in land conservation, especially through the creation of land trusts. Works with ranchers to conserve rural land. https://www.landtrustalliance.org

Horse Trainer.

Horse Trainer

Career Compasses

Get your bearings on what it takes to be a successful horse trainer.

Relevant Knowledge of how to effectively and safely train horses and, more importantly, their owners (40%)

Caring about horses is an absolute necessity. You must really love horses (30%)

Communication Skills to impart knowledge effectively to horses and horse owners (20%)

Ability to Manage Stress is important because your clients, both human and equine, will be difficult more often than not (10%)

Destination: Horse Trainer

So you think you are the next Horse Whisperer? You could be, but let's get one thing straight first: It is almost impossible to make a living working exclusively as a horse trainer. It is a lot like acting, where a few people make a stellar living but the majority do not even get by. There are a few superstar trainers like Pat Parelli and Monty Roberts who make a good living and are household names in the horse world, but most are working other jobs on the side to support their horse training habit. The really lucky ones have other jobs in equine-related industries, such as riding, grooming, barn management, veterinary medicine, selling equine-related products, or in services like farrier and massage therapist. Those are all distinct equine professions, but many people in the horse world work multiple jobs. Trainers are more likely to be professional riders, riding instructors, or operate boarding facilities than to hold other equine-related types of jobs because these jobs coordinate best with training.

Essential Gear

Gallop toward an apprenticeship. Most horse trainers get their start as students of an acclaimed master of their discipline. Find out if the trainer of your choice accepts live-in students. Working pupils often receive room and board in exchange for barn work. More advanced pupils may be given horses to train and exercise or riders to teach in addition to receiving instruction from the master. A lot of this learning takes place by observation rather than in direct one-on-one lessons; the key is to be in proximity to the master and to watch him or her work. Later, you can parlay this connection into a selling point with clients, in essence having a name or brand behind you. Taking on an apprenticeship requires geographical flexibility as you may have to move to wherever your trainer is based, even if it is abroad. It also requires an ability to live frugally in spartan quarters, devoting your days to your work and training. It is a hard life, but rewarding if you really love horses.

While we are bursting bubbles, let us get another one popped before we move on: Most trainers cannot afford to own their own horse farm. Trainers are sometimes employed on large, expensive horse farms in full time jobs that come with accommodations and free board for a horse or two of their own. But they do not earn enough as trainers to purchase their own horse farm on their income from training. If you already own your own horse farm, you have an advantage provided there are sufficient potential clients in your area. If you do not own your own horse farm but want to, do not count on training horses as a viable way to earn the money to purchase it. In the modern world horses are a luxury, and most people involved with horses have to earn the money to support their horse habit in another field altogether. There are full time trainers who make a good living, but they are as rare as actors who win an Academy Award. They are the most well known, but they are a tiny, elite minority.

If these financial drawbacks do not discourage you, it is time to talk more specifically about what a horse trainer does and how you can become one.

At the most basic level, horse trainers teach horses to perform the tasks that people want them to execute, and they help rid horses of behavior that is undesirable to humans. Some horse trainers specialize in working with young horses, teaching them basic commands that allow people to handle them for a variety of purposes such as grooming, shoeing, and veterinary care. Trainers of young horses also "back" them (the term of choice today, supplanting "break") for getting them used to a bridle, saddle, and rider. Trainers almost always specialize in one riding discipline, such as hunt seat, dressage, saddle seat, trick training, or the racing industry. Some horse trainers also teach horses to drive. No, not the family Volvo—they teach them to pull a carriage, sleigh, cart, or, for harness racing, a sulky. Still other trainers do specialized advanced training with horses that show proficiency in such things as dressage and show jumping. These trainers are often successful riders in these disciplines. Finally, a growing category of horse trainer works with horses with specific problems, usually correcting previous training errors and sometimes working with horses that have suffered injuries, abuse, or psychological trauma. You would be surprised how much of the training industry revolves around owners hiring trainers to undo the mistakes of past trainers and re-train their horses.

Most horse training these days is done humanely, but there are some exceptions. The racing industry and some Western disciplines feature horses ridden in races or competition at an age too young to carry a rider. Horses in these disciplines often suffer from chronic injuries later in life due to having been ridden too early and, occasionally, even die during racing or training when their young bones snap under the strain of their work. If you seek to become a trainer in a discipline where horses are ridden too young (defined as before the ages of 3 to 5 years, depending upon the breed), be aware that you are contributing to their potential breakdown in their later years.

Another exception to the norm of modern humane training methods is saddle seat training. The high-stepping action of horses shown in the saddle seat discipline is achieved by the use of caustic ointments, rubber tubing, weights, pulleys, rope, and chains used by trainers. "Soring" is technically illegal, but the laws are not enforced and inhumane training methods are ubiquitous within this discipline. Although certain breeds of horses have a natural high-stepping action, the entire discipline of saddle seat riding is tainted by cruelty of its historic origins. No equine discipline is exempt from animal cruelty, but more humane techniques have crept into some disciplines faster than into others. It is your moral imperative as a horse trainer to ensure that your training methods are cruelty-free, whatever your chosen discipline.

Among the recent styles of training to gain popularity is the so-called natural horsemanship model. Natural horsemanship is a training philosophy that can be used for any discipline. It involves the use of communication techniques between trainer and horse that are based on the horse's natural instincts as a social herd animal. A trainer using natural horsemanship techniques seeks to obtain their horse's willing cooperation by engaging the horse's mind in the task at hand and using a lot of liberty work. Natural horsemanship is a positive development in horse training because it replaces the mentality of "breaking" the horse's spirit with a concept of a positive partnership in which the trainer seeks to understand and work with the horse's natural instincts. It has received criticism for being cultlike, in the sense that certain prominent practitioners have developed followings that condemn all other training methods, and for being gimmicky

Essential Gear

Cash in on your equine industry connections. A key to getting any kind of freelance work, whether you are a horse trainer or a web designer, is networking. Someone who has seen you and your horses at shows or races, or someone who has seen other horses that you have trained, is more likely to hire you to train his or her horses than a stranger. If you hope to train in a competitive discipline, build a name for yourself as a show rider first. Ideally, you should be showing your own horses that you have trained, and their victories will build up demand for your training services. If you cannot afford horses of your own, you need to somehow get work as a professional rider. Winning competitions as a rider is almost as good as winning them as a trainer in terms of building your reputation in the field.

and over-commercialized because these practitioners sell an endless plethora of overpriced videos, books, and gadgets. If you have enough money to pay for their exorbitantly priced programs, you can become a certified trainer in the methodology of one of the famous practitioners, such as Clint Anderson, John Lyons, or Pat Parelli. But bear in mind that such a specialization will close certain doors even as it opens others. Just as the devotees condemn outsiders, most mainstream horse trainers are fairly scathing in their opinion of the natural horsemanship crowd.

You Are Here

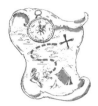

You can begin your journey to horse training from many different locales.

Do you work in a related field? Many horse trainers are also riding instructors, and some start out as exercise riders, professional riders, or grooms. Horse trainers rely primarily on reputation and word of mouth to get clients, so the more connections you have in the horse world, the better. A horse trainer gains respect primarily on the basis of experience, so the longer you have worked with horses, the better your chances of gaining the trust of potential clients. No one wants to be a trainer's first client any more than they want to be a dentist's first patient. The horse world is relatively small, and your reputation will both precede and follow you throughout your career in horse training.

Navigating the Terrain

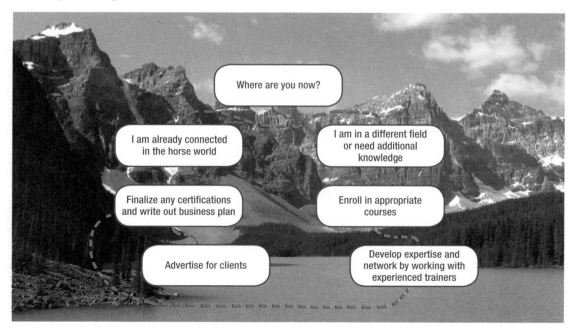

Where are you now?

I am already connected in the horse world

I am in a different field or need additional knowledge

Finalize any certifications and write out business plan

Enroll in appropriate courses

Advertise for clients

Develop expertise and network by working with experienced trainers

Notes from the Field

Suzanne Marshall
Classical dressage trainer
Blairstown, New Jersey

What were you doing before you decided to change careers?

I was an actress. I was in a major soap opera for quite a while, and a variety of other TV shows, among other jobs.

Why did you change your career?

A couple of reasons:

1. The horses simply became too important in my life and I was being asked to choose between my horses and accepting acting jobs away from home. When I started turning down jobs because I didn't want to leave the horses I knew it was time for a change.

2. I got tired of thinking about myself all the time. Acting is a very self involved profession and frankly it got boring always worrying about what I looked like or if I got too fat or if I broke a nail or whatever. The acting itself was fun but the rest of it was a drag. I found much more satisfaction with the horses. I felt much more fulfilled.

How did you make the transition?

I bought a small farm in New Jersey and commuted into New York to do small acting jobs such as industrials and the like. I then started sing-

Do you have an animal-related degree? There is no degree offered in horse training, and no nationally recognized certification or licensing program, but a degree in stable management or equine husbandry or another animal-related field might lend you some credibility in the crucial early phase of getting a job at an equine facility or building a private client base. Once you have established a network of satisfied clients, business will come by word of mouth, and a degree will not matter at all.

Can you work part time? Building up a steady flow of clients neighing at your front door is going to take some time. How are you going

ing at night to keep the performing up. Then as the horse business got too busy I stopped going into the city and quit singing.

What are the keys to success in your new career?

1. My passion. I truly love what I do and bring a passion, intensity and joy to it that attracts people to what I do.

2. There is a uniqueness in what I do. There are other trainers and riding teachers—in fact many, many others—but there are none that I have found in the area (within many hours' drive) that teach what I teach in the manner I teach it. I believe to be successful you can't just be good, you have to have something that sets you apart.

3. Hard, hard work. I have spent years and many, many hours working my tail off for my business. It hasn't always been easy and at times you wonder why the heck you are doing it. But I love what I do and it is worth it. Hard work really does pay off.

4. My calmness. I do not panic easily, I do not get mad easily, I do not overreact. When things go wrong (which trust me they will) I have the ability to calmly assess the situation and take whatever actions I need to remedy it. I believe being able to keep your head and stay calm is critical to success in any field.

to support yourself until your training business supports you? If you can retain your current job, and begin by training in the mornings and on weekends, you may find the financial transition smoother.

Horses usually do not like being worked in the evenings, but that may be the only time available on workdays. If your current job has flexible hours or the option of telecommuting, even better. If you will be traveling to other barns to train, and especially if you will be teaching riders as well as training their horses, you will find that being available at times convenient for your potential clients is crucial to gaining business.

Trainers work when their animals need them.

Organizing your Expedition

Before you set out, know where you are going.

Decide on a destination. What kind of horse trainer would you like to be? You can specialize in Western or English riding, driving, or in a ground training philosophy that can be applied to any discipline. You can work in the racing industry, on the show circuit, or with horses used for pleasure rather than competition. Each discipline is subdivided; for example, dressage trainers can embrace modern or classical dressage. Dressage trainers have usually studied under a master of the art, and are said to be of that "school" of training. These masters can be in the French, German, or other traditions. You could be, for example, a trainer of classical dressage of the French style as taught by the master Nuno Oliveira. Hunt seat riders can specialize in hunters, jumpers, equitation, or eventing (which involves dressage). Western riding has a host of specialties, some derived from traditional ranch work, such as calf roping, and other timed competitive sports such as barrel racing and pole bending. The Western show circuit also includes classes in Western pleasure and equitation. Horse racing can be subdivided by breed, with thoroughbred racing the most well-known, but Quarter horses and Arabians are also raced.

Scout the terrain. It cannot be repeated too often: Getting work as a horse trainer requires having connections in your area of specialization in the horse industry. You cannot simply hang a shingle and expect horse trailers to pull up and unload clients at your door. What riding disciplines are popular where you live? Western riding, as you might expect, is more widespread in the Western states, and English riding dominates in the East. Florida and Kentucky are the two predominant states for the equine industry, in particular, show jumping, eventing, and thoroughbred racing. Many wealthy racing and showing barns in the north winter in Florida each year so they can train uninterrupted by the weather. If you are serious about becoming a horse trainer, you might have to move if there is not enough work in your current locale in your area of expertise. Check local tack shops for advertisements and go to local shows and breed expos to get a sense of what disciplines are most active in your region.

Find the path that's right for you. Consider, above all, your financial situation. A horse trainer is usually a freelance consultant, an independent contractor who usually has no guarantee of another horse to train when the current one trots out the barn door. You may need to juggle marketing yourself with doing the actual training, which can be a difficult balance to strike on your own. You will be unlikely to have benefits or paid vacation time, and scheduling training to suit your clients' schedules will be paramount for building a good reputation in the business. Do you need health insurance? Can you afford to live on part time wages while you are starting out and building your client base? The answers to these questions will help you set out on the right path.

Go back to school. As noted above, there are no particular degree or certification requirements for horse trainers. You are unlikely to have to go back to school to enter this field; however, you do need considerable experience working with all kinds of horses, with a variety of behavioral issues, fears, and past training methods. Although you may not need to attend classes, you definitely need to have worked with horses in some capacity for many, many years, or assist a more experienced trainer, before striking out on your own. If you decide that you want to train horses for the racing industry, you may need to work your way up by starting out as an exercise rider or groom or, if you are small enough, as a jockey.

Landmarks

If you are in your twenties . . . You are a bit young to gain the trust of clients as a trainer, unless you are lucky enough to have been raised on a horse farm and have over a decade of solid training experience under your belt already. If you are still in school, you can major in equine studies and compete in intercollegiate equestrian sports. Even if you are out of school, you may be living at home or have the flexibility to live with roommates, both options that will enable you to accept a lower salary as you build up clientele. This is also a great age to get an entry-level job in a related field, such as becoming a professional rider or groomer or getting into a working pupil arrangement.

If you are in your thirties or forties . . . Think about the financial sacrifice that accompanies life as a professional horse trainer. Can you put your life in storage and move to a small apartment above a barn? Would it be humiliating to be among the "help" on a wealthy estate? If you have a farm where you can board horses that come to you for training, or you can journey to clients' barns, you might find that you can develop horse training as a side-line occupation at first. You may not be able to train full time, but part time experience can help you hitch up toward a career change on the horizon.

If you are in your fifties . . . It is likely that you have some related equine experience, such as raising and training horses on an amateur basis. Now you want to leave your current field and see if your can parlay your training experience into a full time career. If you are lucky, you are contemplating this because enough people are asking you to train their horses that you do not have time to do that and continue at your current job. See if you can shift to part time work as you build up your client base.

Animal work can entail humble dwellings.

If you are over sixty . . . You may have the time freedom and financial wherewithal to take up horse training and see how it goes. If you are re-tired, then some of the pressure may be off of you to make a living from training. You might be able to afford to train at discounted rates or on an amateur basis at first to help you establish your reputation. Experience is an asset so you won't find age discrimination in this business. On the contrary, it will lend you credibility, especially if you have studied with deceased masters of your discipline.

Further Resources

U. S. Horse Trainer   A directory of horse trainers. The site also provides common forms and other resources for professional horse trainers. Site is maintained by trainers who have compiled practical advice based upon their experience in the business. http://www.ushorsetrainer.com
Tellington TTouch Training   A positive training method based on circular movements of the fingers and hands used on horses as well as other animals. The site contains information about obtaining training to become a Ttouch practitioner. http://www.ttouch.com

Natural Horse People   A general natural horsemanship site that contains information about training as well as holistic veterinary care, barefoot trimming and other topics related to natural horse care. http://www.naturalhorsepeople.com

United States Equestrian Federation   The national governing body for equestrian sport, regulating 28 breeds and disciplines and the U.S. teams that compete internationally. http://www.usef.org

Fishing Vessel Operator

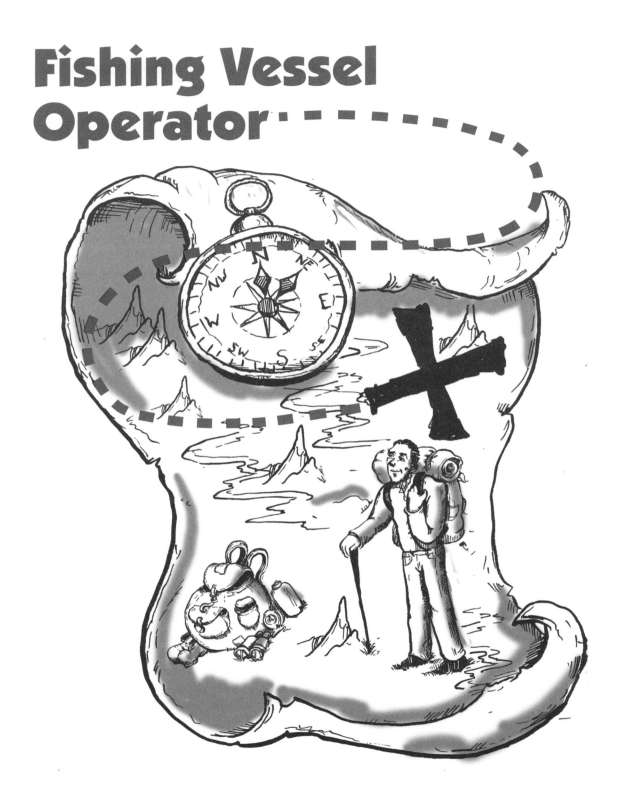

Fishing Vessel Operator

Career Compasses

Get your bearings on what it takes to be a successful fishing vessel operator.

Relevant Knowledge of how to effectively and safely operate a fishing vessel (40%)

Caring about the marine environment is important to sustaining your livelihood (20%)

Communication Skills are useful for working with the other fishermen on your crew (20%)

Ability to Manage Stress is important because the sea is dangerous and unpredictable (20%)

Destination: Fishing Vessel Operator

So you feel the call of the sea, do you matey? You are not alone. The sea has exerted a siren call on man for millennia. It inspired generations of intrepid explorers to investigate what was beyond the horizon until the entire globe was mapped and conquered. Today, an ocean view adds thousands to your property value, and cruises are a popular vacation option. Sailing and fishing remain coveted pastimes because of their relaxation value combined with a frisson of adventure. Commercial fishing, it must be stressed, is not a relaxing pastime. It is a physically arduous, rough, and dangerous job. But that does not mean you would not enjoy it. There is a part of human nature that responds positively to hard, physical labor and you may find it more fulfilling than sitting in a cubicle or behind the wheel of a truck or the counter of a store all day.

Obviously, fishing vessel operators catch fish, but they do not sit in a small boat with a rod and reel. No, fishing vessel operators catch fish and other marine life on a grand scale, using traps, nets, harpoon guns, and other equipment. Most of the catch is for human consumption, but some of it may be used for bait, fertilizer, or animal feed. Commercial fishing vessels do not operate in lakes, rivers, streams, ponds, or other bodies of water where you might go on a solo fishing expedition to catch dinner. These enormous boats fish in the oceans, sometimes hundreds of miles from the nearest shore, well out of sight of any land. They are capable of carrying tens of thousands of pounds of fish or other marine creatures back to shore to be processed. Running a vessel this large requires an entire crew, each member of which has specific duties. Everyone on the crew must work together skillfully and efficiently for the work to proceed safely and in a timely manner. The captain is in charge of the entire expedition. He or she decides where the boat will go, depending upon what species of fish or other marine life are sought, so the captain must have a thorough knowledge of where the best fishing grounds are to be found. To plot the vessel's course to the fishing ground of choice, the captain must be able to use traditional, old-fashioned navigational equipment such as compasses, charts, and, yes, even stars, and he or she

Essential Gear

Pack your suitcase for all seasons. Commercial fishing and sport fishing are both seasonal work. Most fishing vessel operators have other jobs in the off-season. You could fish off the coast of California in the summers and teach skiing in Colorado in the winters. The physical nature of fishing vessel work makes you an ideal candidate for an active, outdoor job in the off-season. You could look elsewhere in this volume for tips on becoming an outdoor sports instructor or adventure travel guide. Of course, after all of that hard labor, you may prefer to spend the off-season in an indoor job. There are a number of Internet and media-related jobs that you can do from the comfort of your home office or anywhere you take your laptop. Flexible and portable off-season employment will be more convenient to work around the availability of fishing jobs.

must be familiar with modern electronic navigational equipment such as GPS. The captain will use radar and sonar to know when he or she has found the fish he or she is seeking. These devices prevent the ship from running into objects hidden under water, not to mention other boats. They are the eyes of the ship when visibility is poor. The amount, quality, and sophistication of equipment vary considerably from vessel to vessel. The captain will also decide what method of capture is to be used, how long the boat will be out to sea, and where and how the catch will be sold when the expedition returns to shore. Fish can be sold directly to wholesalers and processors, or it can go through a fish auction. As with most other types of businesses, the Internet has affected the fishing industry. Many vessels today have Internet on board, which the captain can use to sell the catch directly to consumers, restaurant buyers, and markets, bypassing the wholesalers, processors, and other middlemen.

The captain is responsible for the safety of the crew, so he or she must ensure the seaworthiness of the vessel before each fishing expedition, and must purchase and inspect all of the supplies and equipment that are used on the voyage. There is a lot of gear on a commercial fishing vessel, including netting, cables, and fuel. All must be stowed safely and efficiently. Another important detail to which the captain must attend is the obtainment of all necessary fishing permits and licenses. The captain is required, legally and by tradition, to record the daily activities on board in the ship's log. The captain chooses the other crewmembers who will accompany him or her on the vessel. He or she checks their qualifications and assigns them to appropriate roles and duties on board and also contracts with each crewmember so that he or she receives a portion of the proceeds from the sale of the catch. Please reread that sentence. Remember that the crew are not paid an hourly wage, nor are they on salary. A commercial fisherman gets a portion of the profits from the catch—the lower the catch, or a poor price at market, and the crew earns less.

The next person down in the ship's hierarchy is the first mate. This crew member is the second in command, and takes on the captain's role whenever the captain is off duty. The first mate must be able to perform all of the captain's work, including using the navigation equipment. The first mate's main role is to direct the day-to-day fishing operations on board the vessel and ensure that it is well-maintained and in good repair. The boatswain (sometimes called the deckboss) oversees the work of the deckhands. He or she has the lowest-level supervisory role, but may have to get dirty helping the deckhands load equipment and supplies before the vessel sets sail. He or she may also assist them with their ongoing duties of operating and repairing all of the fishing gear, hauling in the catch, and stowing it. Once the nets and lines are pulled in and the catch is on board, the deckhands must wash it, pack it in ice, and sometimes salt it. They are also responsible for unloading it once the vessel is back in port. Larger, more modern boats sometimes have facilities on board for processing the catch and preparing it for direct sale to consumers, shops, and restaurants. These larger boats can undertake much longer voyages than smaller fishing vessels, and go into deeper water out of sight of land.

Although the vast majority of fishing vessel operators work in the commercial fishing industry, a small number operate boats that are used for sport or recreational fishing. Some captains own smaller vessels that can be hired by private parties for fishing expeditions. These types of expeditions are popular with vacationers in areas with high coastal tourism. This is an option to consider if you are thinking of changing careers into the commercial fishing industry, since employment in this sector is declining rapidly and projected to continue to decrease. Many of the technological innovations cited above that have made commercial fishing more efficient have depleted fish stocks faster than they can replenish themselves.

You Are Here

You can begin your journey to fishing vessel operating from many different locales.

Do you have related experience? When you seek work in a field where employment opportunities are declining rapidly, you have to have considerable experience to attract the attention of potential employers. They are not going to want to invest the money to train inexperienced neophytes when they have their pick of out-of-work regulars who know what they are doing. Since you are changing careers, think hard about what relevant experience you can carry over from your current line of work, your background, or your hobbies. Any fishing or boating experience would be useful, as would familiarity with electronic navigation equipment and the repair and maintenance of fishing vessels and gear.

Do you have a high tolerance for hard, physical labor? Hanging out on a fishing boat in the ocean and getting paid to fish all day long may sound idyllic, but the reality is hardly relaxing. Loading the vessel before departure is extremely heavy work, as is operating the equipment on board, manipulating the catch, cleaning as you go, and unloading when you return to port. Conditions on board may include extreme cold, wind and rain, and unexpected repairs may require improvisation and mechanical aptitude. You must possess great physical strength and stamina and be in hearty good health to contemplate this career choice.

Do you work well with others? Everyone on board a commercial fishing vessel must be able to work together as a team. The operation of a large vessel and the fishing equipment it carries cannot be done by one person alone. It takes good coordination, trust, and communication for the expedition to run smoothly. Good teamwork not only increases productivity, but could be lifesaving in bad weather or in the event of an equipment malfunction.

Navigating the Terrain

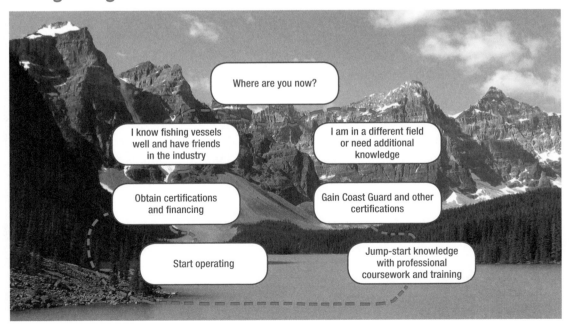

Where are you now?

I know fishing vessels well and have friends in the industry

I am in a different field or need additional knowledge

Obtain certifications and financing

Gain Coast Guard and other certifications

Start operating

Jump-start knowledge with professional coursework and training

Stories from the Field

Frank Mundus
Shark fisherman/Charter boat operator
Montauk (Long Island), New York

No one who has seen *Jaws* will ever forget how shark hunter Captain Quint met his extremely violent and gory end in the mouth of an enormous great white shark. You might be surprised to hear that the character of Quint was based on a real person. Frank Mundus ran a charter fishing operation based out of Montauk harbor on the South Fork of Long Island from 1951 until his death on September 10, 2008. He did not start out as a shark specialist, or even as a fisherman at all. He grew up in Brooklyn and dropped out of high school, first finding work as a freight handler. As a child, he had broken his left arm. It failed to heal properly and his parents took him swimming to strengthen it. Thus began a lifelong love affair with the sea. His love of the ocean drew him to find a job working on charter boats, for a wage unthinkable now: $3 per day. Eventually Mundus bought his own boat, which he named *Cricket* because people told him he resembled that character from *Pinocchio*. He took fishermen out to catch mackerel and bluefish until, one

Organizing your Expedition

Before you set out, know where you are going.

Decide on a destination. As noted previously, job prospects in this industry are declining. More than 38,000 individuals were employed in the commercial fishing industry in 2006 and that number is expected to decline approximately 16 percent to 32,000 by 2016. But there will be some job openings due to attrition and retirement. Workers leave the profession frequently due to the hazardous working conditions and the physical strain and boredom of the work. The seasonal nature of the work, with its lack of steady, year-round income is also a major reason for attrition. These facts can help guide you in your search for work. Consider whether you want to work on a large fishing vessel, where labor is *day, sharks were so plentiful that he hauled one on board. From that day forward, he specialized in what he termed, "monster fishing," and he was called the "Monster Man" for his interest in catching sharks and his ability to drag in large ones. In 1964, he caught a 17-and-a-half foot, 4,500-pound great white, the largest ever caught. His reputation began to spread, and he stoked it with his pirate-like appearance and unusual hands-on technique. At the age of 81 he caught a nine-footer, with a rod and reel, not a harpoon. In 1991, he and his wife moved to Hawaii, but he returned each summer to take tourists on expensive shark hunts in his boat, the Cricket II. The real shark hunter's end was less dramatic than Captain Quint's: After spending the night on his boat on the last day of the fishing season, he flew back to Hawaii and collapsed of a heart attack upon arrival.*

Several features of the Monster Man's career trajectory are relevant to career changers today. First, he took a low paid, entry-level job to get into his desired field. Next, he saw what he needed to do for advancement—buy a boat—and he worked diligently and singlemindedly in pursuit of that goal. Finally, he took advantage of the opportunity to carve his own niche, specializing in one type of very lucrative charter tour.

more highly specialized, or a smaller vessel, with just a few men who divide all types of work between them. The one area of the industry that is not experiencing declining employment prospects is sport fishing. If you have a boat that you can hire out for charter expeditions, this might be the way forward to your new career. If you lack a boat as of yet, look for jobs that are linked to boating and fishing as tourism rather than industrial fishing.

Scout the terrain. As you would expect, the commercial fishing industry is concentrated along the coasts. New England has the oldest industry, but fish stocks have also declined most rapidly here. The Gulf Coast is home to a sizable segment of the industry, as is the Pacific coast off California, and Alaska. Pacific fish stocks have not been depleted as much as Atlantic ones, and the most fish caught by volume takes place in Alaska. If you do not live in one of these areas, take heart. Some commercial fishing is based off of the Southeastern seaboard, in states such as Virginia, and sport fishing takes place just about everywhere you find tourists.

Find the path that's right for you. Consider above all your financial situation. Commercial fishing is not a well-paying occupation. The average earnings of fishermen as of May 2006 were only $27,250. The bottom 10 percent earned considerably less, below $15,280, and the top 10 percent of earners were just over $45,480. Remember, the work is not year-round; the work is seasonal. It is usually full time during the fishing season, primarily summer and fall in most regions, but it can be part time even in-season in areas where overfishing has brought the industry into decline. The right job for you is one that enables you to earn enough to survive in the off-season, and one whose schedule fits around your off-season employment.

Essential Gear

Make sure the middle name on your passport is "Danger." The working conditions on a fishing vessel are some of the most hazardous and unpleasant in all industries. Living quarters are close and smelly, and there are few amenities. Malfunctioning equipment or bad weather can lead to collisions, shipwrecks, and drowning or serious injuries. Crew members can be swept overboard or slip in wet or icy conditions, and medical treatment is not readily at hand in the event of an injury. Entanglement in nets, ropes, and other equipment is a constant danger, and sometimes your catch can bite, sting, or thrash you. Boredom is another danger of this job, with your time split between furious activity and interminable waiting.

Go back to school. Most fishing vessel operators acquire their skills on the job. It is an industry in which families are likely to be involved for generations, so that you are born into it and have family connections to help you get your foot on the deck, so to speak. You are unlikely to have to go back to school to enter this field; however, you do need Coast Guard certification to operate a large commercial fishing vessel and you must complete a Coast Guard-approved training course in order to obtain it. See the Coast Guard Web links at the end of this chapter for more information on how to enroll in these courses. Some colleges and universities located in coastal areas offer programs in seamanship that include navigational skills, vessel maintenance and repair, and fishing technology. The Coast Guard Academy is located in New London, Connecticut, and cadets can cross-register for courses at nearby Connecticut College. But bear in mind that the academy is extremely selective in its admissions. The Merchant Institute, Inc., in Southern California, offers courses that can open doors to a wide variety of maritime professions, useful if you would like your skill set to be transferable beyond commercial fishing: http://www.mmts.com. If you prefer to be on the East Coast, consider the Massachusetts Maritime Academy: http://www.maritime.edu.

Landmarks

If you are in your twenties . . . You may have family connections or a lifelong love of the sea that are prompting you towards a career as a fishing vessel operator. You don't need a specific degree to enter this field but, if you are still in school, you can major in a maritime specialty. Apply to join the U.S. Coast Guard, or transfer to one of the maritime colleges. You can also seek summer employment on fishing vessels whilst you are a student. It is the ideal summer job for this career choice. Even if you are out of school, you may be living at home or have the flexibility to live with roommates, both options that will enable you to accept the lower earnings of seasonal employment. You are also likely to be healthy and fit at this age, and to have more geographic and seasonal flexibility.

If you are in your thirties or forties . . . You must be feeling the call of the sea strongly if you are seriously contemplating leaving a full time job for the vagaries of life as a seasonal independent contractor. If you are a teacher or have a seasonal job already, you may be better placed to begin fishing as a career. Or perhaps you live on a heavily touristed coast and you see a potential market for boat tours. If you have your own vessel, find out everything you need to get started as a licensed boat tour operator in your locality. Then, anchors away.

If you are in your fifties . . . Unless you have been in a poorly paid field for most of your working life, the move to fishing as a career is likely to involve a substantial pay cut. Ask yourself if you can afford to live on a fisherman's wages, and how the projected decline of the industry may affect your retirement savings and plans.

If you are over sixty . . . You may have the time and financial freedom to enter this field. The seasonal nature of the job and the unpredictability of the earnings may not be a problem for you if you are well-placed financially at this stage of your life. Nor are the long-term projections for decline in the industry likely to be an impediment for you. Your biggest obstacles are likely to be physical. The fact that the job involves hard, manual labor means that you are likely to face age discrimination on the job market. Your best bet is to go into the field of sport fishing rather than commercial fishing at this stage of life. If you have your own boat, get yourself set up to offer expeditions for tourists and sportsmen.

Further Resources

Coast Guard Office of Compliance for Commercial Fishing Vessels A site maintained by the Department of Transportation that lists legal requirements for commercial fishing vessels.
http://www.access.gpo.gov/nara/cfr/waisidx_01/46cfr28_01.html

National Maritime Center (NMC) A site maintained by the U.S. Coast Guard that contains information on Mariner Licensing and Documentation (MLD). http://www.uscg.mil/nmc

United States Coast Guard Official recruiting site with information on careers with the Coast Guard and Coast Guard Reserve.
http://www.gocoastguard.com

VetSuccess.gov A site maintained by the U.S. Department of Veteran Affairs that provides information on how to launch a career as a fishing vessel operator. http://www.vetsuccess.gov/resources/occupations/profile?id=257

Adventure
Travel Guide

Adventure Travel Guide

Career Compasses

Get your bearings on what it takes to be a successful adventure travel guide.

Relevant Knowledge of how to safely lead inexperienced trekkers around your terrain (30%)

Caring about the environment is an absolute necessity, otherwise the tourists you guide can damage the ecosystem (20%)

Communication Skills are the most vital skill set for this job as it involves dealing with many different types of people and ensuring they follow directions for their own safety (20%)

Ability to manage stress is important because your clients will be difficult, stupid, or both, more often than not (30%)

Destination: Adventure Travel Guide

If you like to travel and you have been searching for an outdoor career that will not feel like work, you may be happy as an adventure travel guide. Travel guides lead groups of tourists on sight-seeing trips that may last a few hours and be confined to one museum or that may last weeks and traverse an entire country or region. Adventure travel guides are a specific subset of travel guides who lead tourists on outdoor expeditions, often in exotic locales and over difficult terrain.

Adventure travel guides are employed everywhere there are tourists, so possible job locations are limited only by your tastes and skills. American tourists typically stick close to home when they travel, with Mexico the top foreign tourism destination, followed by Canada. When Americans head to Europe, they most often visit the United Kingdom, followed by France and Germany. Although there are some adventure travel opportunities in all of these destinations, such as horseback riding holidays in France and hiking journeys in the United Kingdom and Germany, you can find many adventure travel employment options both here at home and in exotic locales around the world. The United States is so climatologically and geographically diverse that each of the 50 states has some land or water feature that facilitates exploration with a trained guide. Wilderness adventure can be found not just in the ice floes of Alaska or the volcanic valleys of Hawaii, but even on sea-kayaking expeditions off the coast of Rhode Island or tramping through the woods of Maryland. The fact that you can work most anywhere makes this an appealing career choice whether you want to stick close to home or travel as far away as possible. The number of outdoor activities for which you can lead tour groups is enticingly large and varied. On land you can explore caves, ruins, fossils, and other vestiges of the past. You can lead mountain climbers, hikers, skiers, horseback riders, bikers, runners, and wildlife spotters. On the water, you can take tourists canoeing, kayaking, white-water rafting, sailing, and fishing. In the water, you can cliff dive, snorkel, scuba dive, and swim with aquatic wildlife such as dolphins, whales, and sharks. (Note that health insurance may be harder to obtain with that last option!)

Although spending your working hours as you would your free time—out in nature hiking, biking, skiing, or boating—may be what draws you to the job, you should know that much of an adventure travel guide's work takes place before and after the tour, behind the scenes. For some packaged tours, the arrangements are made by a travel agency or travel program. The guide is hired for a specific expedition. Often the guide is responsible not only for leading the tour, but for making all travel arrangements for the participants including transportation, lodging, meals, and other activities besides the outdoor portion of the trip, as well as taking care of obtaining permits, visas, vaccinations, supplies, equipment, and other pre-departure details. The guide must also ensure the suitability and preparation of group participants for the activities in which they will engage. Preparing packing lists and medical questionnaires to be distributed to the group members before departure is another important part of the job. Halfway up the mountain is a bit late to find out that half your group didn't bring flashlights, the other half has no warm clothes, and Mr. Jones has asthma but no inhaler in his rucksack.

Once the pre-departure work is finished, your real work begins. Unless you are leading an expedition where it is stipulated that the participants be skilled and experienced in the activity—for example, leading an endurance ride in which the participants bring their own endurance horses, a scuba dive holiday for advanced divers, or a mountain climbing expedition for experienced climbers—you will have to give the group members some basic instruction in how to use their equipment and navigate the terrain before you set off. You are, of course, fully responsible for the safe return of everyone in your group, and illness, accident, and injury will be constant worries when you are out with your charges. You will have to inform them of dangers from snakes, insects, poisonous plants, or other threats to their safety, as well as instruct them in any local customs to which they must adhere, not to mention proper environmental stewardship in the "take nothing but pictures, leave nothing but footprints" vein.

Essential Gear

A good reputation is your passport to success. If travelers enjoy the adventure they experienced under your guidance, they are likely to recommend it to others. They might also praise you to the owners of the company, either on evaluation forms or personal letters and e-mails. Good recommendations from group members can help you to get rehired next season or help you secure work elsewhere. Likewise, negative reviews from tourists will affect your standing with your employer, even if the conditions that ruined their holiday, such as the weather, were out of your control. Do everything within your power short of outright bribery to win over your groups and get them to like you. Your job depends upon it.

A secondary goal on some expeditions may be to spot wildlife or for the participants to learn a new skill. Your group must also have a good dynamic to be successful, with everyone working together cooperatively. Since the group will often be strangers to one another—or worse, family members—it can sometimes be hard to get personality types and learning styles to mesh well. You will wear many hats as travel planner, tour guide, educator, nurse, and psychologist. It is really a profession with several jobs rolled into one, and the skill set to be a successful adventure tour guide is unusually broad. Ideally, you should be certified to teach your activity of choice and have some teaching experience before you become a guide. You must also have considerable environmental knowledge in order to protect the habitat in which you lead adventurers and to follow local nature protection laws. Ecotourism is a growing area of adventure travel, especially in Costa Rica and other developing tropical areas. First Aid knowledge and some type of CPR certification will be required by most legitimate employers. You should also be familiar with the region, both to answer questions posed by tourists, and to offer useful information for safety and enjoyment. Knowledge of the geological history of the area, and the wildlife that inhabit it, will come in handy as well.

Finally, you must really love people. You will be dealing with a great variety of them, in situations that will often be new and stressful to them. Physical discomfort and fear, not to mention jet lag or foodborne illness, can often bring out the worst in people. You must project an air of competence, calmness, resourcefulness, trustworthiness, and patience to earn the respect and obtain the cooperation of your groups.

You Are Here

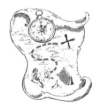

You can begin your journey to becoming an adventure travel guide from many different locales.

Do you work in a related field? Adventure travel guiding is a seasonal job except in the most temperate climates, so you will likely need another job for the off-season. If you currently work as an outdoor sports instructor or in a tourism-related field, this can help you secure employment as an adventure travel guide. Since there are no specific educational requirements, simply being in the right place at the right time can be your ticket to a new job. If you work within the tourism industry, you can use your knowledge and connections to find out about adventure guide openings and be first in line.

Do you know first aid and CPR? Some employers, especially in developing countries, may not have high standards for safety, but most legitimate employers will want to see CPR certification. Wherever you live, you should be able to easily find a CPR training course near you. They are offered by the American Heart Association, the American Red Cross, and by some local fire departments (use the non-emergency number to phone yours and enquire).

What type of tours can you lead? If you are considering leading adventure tours as a career, you probably have some outdoor skill or outdoor sport that you play well. Perhaps you went on a scuba diving holiday in the Caribbean and looked enviously at the instructors, thinking, "Hey, they get to stay on this beautiful sunny island and dive every day and I have to go back to my cold, grey cubicle when this vacation ends." The impulse to become an adventure travel guide often comes from the desire to keep the vacation from ending. That's fine, but you need to have a solid background, not just a holiday's worth of practice, in your adventure of choice.

Navigating the Terrain

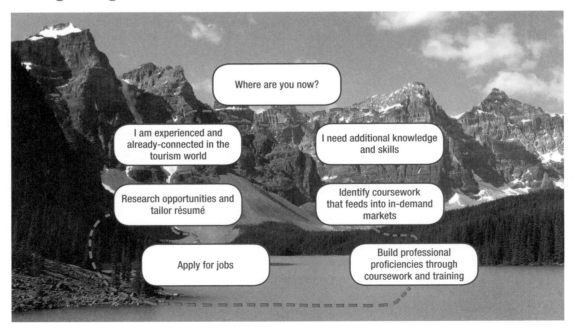

Organizing your Expedition

Before you set out, know where you are going.

Decide on a destination. What kind of adventure travel guide would you like to be? As noted above, there are adventure travel opportunities around the world, in every possible field of outdoor recreation, and new, hybrid sports (such as parasailing and zip-lining) are being invented all the time. As baby boomers retire with better health and fitness than previous generations of retirees who sought more sedentary travel, demand for adventure holidays is expected to increase. Spas and resorts increasingly offer adventure travel options. Some are relatively tame, such as zip lines, parasailing, diving, or snorkeling activities during day stops on a cruise. In this sort of job, you would live on the island and greet each shipload as they came in, guiding those passengers who had signed up in advance for your activity. These expeditions usually last no longer than a few hours, and are rarely strenuous. At the other end of the spectrum are hard-core adventure holidays where travelers rough it in the wilderness for weeks, with only you, the guide, standing between them and death by starvation or exposure.

Scout the terrain. The adventure travel options available in your region are determined by the climate and the natural features of the terrain. If you are in Michigan and you want to lead snorkeling tours of coral reefs, you are going to have to move. (Likewise if you are in Florida and you want to lead cross-country ski adventures.) Beyond those obvious limitations, certain sports and activities are available in many locales, and you will need to look at the links at the end of this chapter to find out where there are current job openings. If you want to live in your new abode year round, find out what employment opportunities exist in the off-season. That is a crucial piece in the puzzle of your adventure travel dream.

Find the path that's right for you. Consider, above all, your financial situation. An adventure travel guide is a seasonal employee, with no guarantee of work in the following year. If the economy is doing poorly, recreational travel may decline, or tourists may gravitate toward less

Notes from the Field

Katie Durbin
Rafting guide
Denver, Colorado

What were you doing before you decided to change careers?

I was a snowboarding instructor. Actually, I will be teaching boarding again this winter. It's a seasonal job, so I usually do that from November to April, and then something else in the off-season.

Why did you change your career?

As I said, I can't honestly say I have changed career. I used to waitress in the summers, but I wanted to work outside. I didn't want to be waitressing forever: the other waitresses are usually college students, and it started to feel weird once I hit thirty. But I didn't want to give up boarding. I could work some other job and still board, but I wouldn't get to do it as often as I do as an instructor.

expensive package deals. If you work in a large resort or for a cruise line that offers a wide variety of activities beyond adventure travel to attract guests, your job may be more secure. In smaller companies, you will be unlikely to have benefits or paid vacation time, although you will most likely be provided with accommodations and paid travel to/from your place of employment each year. Do you need health insurance? It is certainly a good idea when you are engaging in dangerous outdoor sports on a daily basis! Can you afford to live on seasonal wages? Do you have a job or other source of income, such as savings or investments, lined up for the off-season? The answers to these questions will help you set out on the right path.

Go back to school. There are no particular degree requirements or educational qualifications for adventure travel guides beyond demonstrated competence in your sport or activity and CPR/First Aid certification, and for certain activities, such as scuba diving, you may be required to show proof of certification to reputable employers. But bear in mind

How did you make the transition?

I was looking for another seasonal job. I looked into hotel work, but none of the seasonal jobs appealed to me and most did not pay well. I tried working as a night auditor, but it didn't suit me. My boyfriend, also a boarder (naturally!), was working as a rafting guide in the summers. Quite a few boarding and ski instructors do. I went with him on a few trips, then took a training course offered by the Colorado State Parks and Recreation Department.

What are the keys to success in your new career?

I think the biggest challenge is making the trip fun for the rafters. Usually, it's families on vacation, or couples, sometimes groups from work or high school students on Outward Bound. Most have never gone rafting before, and so much of the job involves explaining about safety and making sure everyone has all of their equipment on and understands and follows instructions, that it's hard to remember that we're supposed to be having a good time. I try to be a comedian, make them laugh.

that adventure travel guiding is seasonal work and, unless you are independently wealthy, you will need a second job for the off-season. This is where school could come in handy. If you work at a resort, you could wait tables, perform maintenance or work a desk job during the off-season. With a degree in the hospitality industry, you could be running the place or at least moving up the food chain.

Landmarks

If you are in your twenties . . . You are at an ideal age, both physically and mentally, to begin a career as an adventure guide. Since it is a seasonal job, it works well as summer employment if you are still in school. If you major in a sports or hospitality-industry related field, you can line up a compatible off-season career for yourself.

If you are in your thirties or forties . . . You may have tried a career in the city and discovered that you want to be living the lifestyle on your desktop background rather than at your desk. This may be just the time to make a major move to a new lifestyle, if you can pack up and take off to where the jobs are. Start by lining up a job and trying it for a season, if possible, taking a leave of absence from your career.

Essential Gear

Good judgment is the one item you cannot forget to pack. A museum guide asking herself, "What is the worst that could happen?" is probably thinking of her charges being bored and not liking the artwork or her spiel. In the case of an adventure travel guide, the answer to that query is a bit starker: Your charges could die. The nature of your work involves taking people who are on vacation from their normal lives into an unfamiliar, challenging, and exciting environment. Part of the excitement, whether you are careening through white water rapids on a raft or floating gently down the Amazon, comes from the danger. All adventure holidays come with some sort of built-in danger, whether from falling, drowning, or getting bitten or stung. In order to keep that danger only a theoretical possibility, you need to exercise good judgment at all times.

If you are in your fifties . . . You might be in a good position to exchange the rat race for an endurance ride. If you have a skill that you can parlay into a career as an adventure guide, you could find yourself in demand from older travelers who like the idea of a guide who is closer to their demographic.

If you are over sixty . . . You may have taken some adventure holidays and decided that being an adventure travel guide could be an ideal post-retirement career. If your children are grown and your mortgage paid off, then you could pack up and move to a beach house in Thailand or a Caribbean resort from which you can lead diving expeditions.

Further Resources

GORP.com Site for people interested in adventure travel. It is not specifically geared toward professional adventure travel guides, but information on the site about where to go for adventure travel vacations will be useful for finding employment. http://gorp.away.com/index.html
Adventure Jobs USA An online resource for job seekers. Contains a wide variety of types of jobs from wilderness therapy to environmental

education, both in the United States and worldwide.
http://www.backdoorjobs.com/adventure.html

CruiseJobFinder.com Lists employment opportunities for adventure guides worldwide, with an emphasis on group tours led by guides with local expertise. Not just for cruise ships.
http://www.cruisejobfinder.com/fm/tourguides

Great-Adventures.com Features a global list of organizations that offers employment and volunteer opportunities.
http://www.great-adventures.com/know/plan/work.html

Outdoor Sports Instructor

Outdoor Sports Instructor

Career Compasses

Get your bearings on what it takes to be a successful outdoor sports instructor.

Relevant Knowledge of how to play your sport and teach it to others (40%)

Mathematical Skills for keeping score (10%)

Communication Skills to teach your students/clients effectively (30%)

Ability to Manage Stress so you don't lose your temper when your athlete or team loses (20%)

Destination: Outdoor Sports Instructor

Are you an armchair coach? Do you call plays to the TV set or from the stands and think, "I could do a better job?" Well, here is your chance to find out if you really can. If you are serious about a career change, you could find yourself as the recipient of unsolicited advice from spectators. From kids barely out of diapers learning skills on peewee teams to Olympic-level athletes at the top of their form, all need coaches and instructors to train them in their chosen sport. Depending on your experience, connections, talents, and career goals, you have many types of outdoor sports instructor jobs from which to choose.

First, let's differentiate between sports *coaches* and sports *instructors*. These roles overlap so substantially that it is difficult to distinguish them. Basically, coaches work with teams and sports instructors work with individual athletes; however, individual athletes such as gymnasts who compete together in teams may refer to the team's "coach." Both coaches and sports instructors prepare their athletes for competition by viewing and critiquing the competition's strengths, weaknesses, and strategies, and by developing individual game plans for their team or athletes. Coaches usually confer with their teams before, during, and after games. They can call specific plays and instructions, as well as make changes to the team lineup and strategy as circumstances dictate. Individual instructors are often relegated to the sidelines during competitions. In many sports, they are not allowed to communicate with their charges or offer mid-competition advice. Both coaches and sports instructors take official charge of the equipment that is used by the team or individual athlete. They may have assistance with transporting, maintaining, repairing, and taking inventory of it, but they usually have the final say in which materials and supplies are purchased for their athletes' use. (An exception to this rule is a sponsorship tie with a major company.) Coaches and sports instructors devise training plans and supervise workouts, critiquing the performance of their athletes and giving individual advice to improve form, technique, playing skills, and stamina. They may also advise players on diet, supplements, medication, physical therapy, and massage, and help them seek medical treatment when necessary. Coaches usually have assistants that help run teams through drills and practice plays. Instructors may have assistants as well. Tennis instructors, for example, may have assistants that are assigned to train

Essential Gear

Get into the game. Learn everything you can about the sport you want to teach. Follow it professionally, play it as much as possible, attend clinics with famous players, and read their published tips and technical guides. The more all-around expertise you have, the better for your players. If you coach individual athletes, you will need to spend almost as much time watching the competition as watching your own charges. Keep up with the latest trends in techniques, strategies and tactics, and equipment in your sport.

with their charges, as well as physical therapists, massage therapists, sports psychologists, and other peripheral employees who work regularly with their athletes as part of a training routine. Coaches must also ensure that their team members develop habits of good sportsmanship, maintain team spirit, and diffuse any difficulties in relationships between members of the team that may affect cooperation and success on the field. Sports instructors may have to mediate disputes between individual athletes and foster good sportsmanship and a competitive spirit. They can focus on an individual's strengths and weaknesses more readily than a team coach, and the exercises, drills, and other forms of preparation that they prescribe are completely individualized. Because sports instructors work one-on-one, they sometimes have to play against their charges to facilitate practice of their sport, simulate competition, and demonstrate techniques.

Coaches who work in college or professional level competition are usually employed full time. They are a coach by profession and travel with their teams during the playing season, often spending much time away from their homes and families. In the off-season, they may still have to travel a substantial amount to scout and recruit prospective players. Their working hours can be long and irregular. Preparation for practice begins early in the morning and games often take place at night or on the weekdays. Their job security is usually linked to their team's success and the pressure can cause a variety of stress-related health problems. Coaches at high school level and below are often teachers in academic disciplines who coach on the side for supplementary income. Coaches of children who are not affiliated with schools, such as those for neighborhood and club sports teams, are usually parents of children on the team. Sports instructors at higher levels are almost always retired competitors in that sport, but lower-level instructors may never have launched a successful professional or amateur career. They may not yet be of retirement age for their sport, and some may still be hoping for a competitive career of their own.

If you decide that a career in outdoor sports instruction is right for you, choosing your sport will likely be the easiest move on your playlist. You probably already have a sport in mind for which you believe your expertise as a player would translate into skill as an instructor. If you have played football *and* baseball, or softball *and* soccer, or run cross-country *and* played tennis, you may have to make a choice—but it should not be

too difficult to decide which sport you are better prepared to coach. If you are truly torn, consider the opportunities in your area and let job openings make the decision for you.

The income of outdoor sports instructors varies considerably. Those coaching childrens' or amateur adult teams almost always do so on a voluntary basis, while coaches of top professional teams are awarded glittering contracts in the millions. In May 2006, college/university coaches earned an average salary of $37,530. Those coaching in elementary and secondary schools earned an average of $21,960. In coaching individuals rather than teams, sports instructors are either paid per hour, per session, or per athlete. The rates that you can command will depend upon your reputation, the success of your athletes in competition, and the level at which you teach.

You Are Here

You can begin your journey to becoming an outdoor sports instructor from many different locales.

Are you or were you a competitor in your sport? As noted previously, most coaches and sports instructors are former players. Some had long and stellar careers, others retired young due to injury. There is no correlation between being a winning competitor and being a great coach or instructor. Arsene Wenger, coach of North London's Arsenal Football Club, is one of the most successful coaches at the top level of this highly competitive sport, but he was only a mediocre defender in his playing days. In fact, sometimes less-than-stellar players go on to be top coaches and instructors whose teams and charges win at the highest levels, and some winning athletes fizzle as coaches, never producing successful teams and sometimes leaving the game for other fields entirely. This should not come as a surprise. The skills and talents needed to win as an athlete are quite different than the ones needed to be a successful coach. If the skills for success come too naturally to you, you may not be able to explain them to others. This can be illustrated with an example from the world of—believe it or not—opera singing. One of the most celebrated opera singers in the world today is the New Zealand soprano Dame Kiri Te Kanawa. When asked about her singing technique, she replied, "I just

Navigating the Terrain

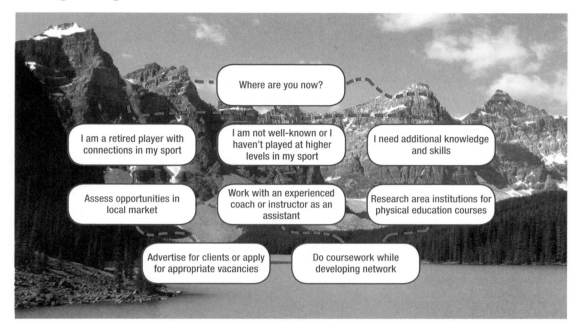

Where are you now?

I am a retired player with connections in my sport

I am not well-known or I haven't played at higher levels in my sport

I need additional knowledge and skills

Assess opportunities in local market

Work with an experienced coach or instructor as an assistant

Research area institutions for physical education courses

Advertise for clients or apply for appropriate vacancies

Do coursework while developing network

open my mouth and the sound comes out." A singer—and, by extension, anyone in any field—who has to *work* at producing the right sounds and *think* about how to do so may be better equipped to explain technical details to students.

Do you have a sports-related degree? A retired player can usually get a coaching or instructing job on the basis of experience alone, but if you are looking to enter coaching in a school or without a career in the sport behind you, you will need something to convince potential clients and employers that you can handle the job. Coaches in the public school system will need to have a bachelor's degree and meet state teaching certification requirements (which vary considerably from state-to-state), but these qualifications may not be necessary in a private school. Many colleges and universities offer degrees in sports-related fields, such as exercise science, sports management, kinesiology, nutrition, physical education, sports psychology, sports medicine, and physical therapy.

Notes from the Field
Dorothy McDermott
Ski instructor
Stowe, Vermont

What were you doing before you decided to change careers?

I'm a plant biologist. Skiing is a seasonal job, so I don't do it year-round. In the summers, I work for the U.S. Geological Survey as a seasonal employee. Last summer I was in Utah cataloging plants, but most years we are out measuring the regrowth after forest fires in California and Arizona.

Why did you change your career and how did you make the transition?

After my first season with the USGS, I decided that I wanted to come back the next summer. I am originally from Vermont, and I had worked as a ski instructor before. I didn't have a permanent home of my own,

Can you work part time? Coaches at the college and professional levels, as well as sports instructors who work with individual athletes at higher levels of amateur and professional competition, usually work full time. But coaches and instructors of K–12 school athletes, of children who take lessons in sports like tennis or skiing, and teams and clubs that are privately owned and operated, usually work only part time, and sometimes on a voluntary basis. To make this career change, you need to know if the job for which you are aiming is full time or part time. If part time, can you survive financially on this income or supplement it from other part time work?

Organizing your Expedition

Before you set out, know where you are going.

Decide on a destination. Your sport will dictate whether you coach a team, such as with baseball or field hockey, or individuals, such as with running or skiing. In some jobs, you may coach a team composed of

so I stayed with my mom and taught skiing that winter. That was five years ago, and I've been doing it ever since, except one year I went with some friends to teach skiing in Colorado instead.

What are the keys to success in your new career?

You need a lot of patience. It sounds great to get to ski all day and get paid for it, but you're mostly running up and down the bunny hill shouting, and demonstrating the same basic stuff over and over. You don't get cold, which is the first thing you'd imagine, but it can get boring and you can't wait for the lesson to end so you can go ski before your next group arrives. A lot of people don't follow directions well, and you have to try to get inside their head and figure out a way to explain how to stop without falling over, or how to turn, in a way that gets through to them. It takes experience, but you always need patience, no matter how much experience you have.

individual competitors, such as a school's tennis or cross-country team. Consider first whether you want to coach children or adults. If you want to instruct children, what age group do you think you can teach effectively and enjoyably? The challenges of teaching children and adults can be quite distinct and your temperament will help dictate your choice. If you decide to instruct young children, remember that children can begin certain sports as young as age three, but that their bodies cannot handle other sports until middle or high school. If you decide to teach children, you also need to determine whether you want to teach in a school or privately at a youth center, municipal sports complex, or camp. Given that most outdoor sports have seasons, you may have to coach in another location or in another sport, or find alternate employment, during the off-season for your sport. If you coach a high school tennis team during the academic year, for example, you might teach at a tennis camp during the summers.

Scout the terrain. As any good coach knows, it takes a little scouting around to find the brightest prospects. That holds true for jobs as well as players. Look at local job listings for vacancies in your area. There are many Web sites that advertise coaching jobs. You can also go directly to sports centers in your area and enquire in person if they are looking for instructors. Businesses that hire seasonal employees, such as tennis facilities and ski resorts, tend to have a high turnover rate and are often looking for new staff. Drop off your résumé well before your sport's season begins.

Essential Gear

Work your connections and advertise. Many jobs in this field are the result of connections and word of mouth. If your snowboarding students like you, they will recommend you to their friends. If you patronize and put up signs in local sports equipment shops advertising your tennis or golf lessons, the employees there may recommend you to customers who ask about local instructors.

Find the path that's right for you. As noted previously, the hours and pay for various types of outdoor sports instructor jobs vary enormously. Your financial situation, as well as your skills, experience, and interests will dictate the road that you should travel in search of your new career. If you lack experience, consider starting with an internship or a volunteer position. Local youth teams are usually in desperate need of volunteer coaches so they are not picky about experience. An unpaid position now may allow you to build the experience and expertise for a paid position later. You may also decide that you would like to keep coaching as a hobby and stay in your current job or pursue a related career in sports management or administration.

Go back to school. If you are a former competitive athlete in your sport, you are unlikely to need to go back to school to get a job, and there may be no clear benefit to doing so. Likewise, if you have considerable volunteer coaching experience, you may be offered a paid position on the strength of your record, reputation, or experience alone. But there are some instances in which returning to school might be professionally useful. If you are seeking a full time position but have little experience, an athletics-related degree might be an asset on the job market. Many colleges and universities offer them, at both the undergraduate and graduate levels. Seattle University offers a Master in Sport Administration and Leadership (MSAL). There is even a school known as the United States Sports Academy that only offers sports-related degrees (check them out at http://www.ussa.edu). A degree is a necessity for many fields that are peripherally related to coaching, such as physical therapy, sports management, sports journalism, and sports administration. Some organizations would be happy to hire a coach with a business-related degree, especially with a concentration in finance, because he or she could assist with fund-raising and organizational management.

Landmarks

If you are in your twenties . . . You might be considering sports instruction because you have not managed to sustain a professional career in your sport or an injury has forced you into early retirement. Perhaps you have graduated college without a professional contract in the offing and you want to remain involved with your sport. Lack of coaching experience may be a problem for you if you are in one of these situations, so try volunteering, looking for internships, going to graduate school for a sports-related degree, or utilizing connections from your playing days.

If you are in your thirties or forties . . . You might have just retired from a career playing your sport. If this is the case, work those connections to get a job, while your name recognition is high and your playing experience is recent.

If you are in your fifties . . . If you are looking at sports instruction as a new career, you have likely not been a competitive player of your sport for some time. This may work against you unless you have substantial related experience, such as an amateur coaching or fitness-related job along the lines of a physical education teacher. Your best move may be to find a volunteer coaching position to build experience for a career move into a more permanent position.

If you are over sixty . . . The advice for those in their fifties applies to you as well. Many coaches work well into their seventies and beyond. But some individual sports instruction jobs are physically demanding and require the instructor be able to play and demonstrate the skills and tactics of that sport. This is not necessarily an impediment, just something of which to be aware.

Further Resources

National Association of Sports Officials is a membership organization for sports officials at all levels and in all sports. Membership includes a subscription to *Referee* magazine. http://www.naso.org

American Sport Education Program provides coaching education courses and other resources. http://www.asep.com

National Alliance for Youth Sports promotes safety in children's sports and educates coaches, parents and administrators on making sports a positive developmental experience. http://www.nays.org

National Council of Youth Sports is a membership organization comprising the "Who's Who" in youth sports. http://www.ncys.org

Plant Nursery Operator

Plant Nursery Operator

Career Compasses

Get your bearings on what it takes to run a successful plant nursery.

Relevant Knowledge of how to grow plants (40%)

Caring about nature enough to have a genuine understanding of ecosystems and how each plant plays a role in the collective planet's health (30%)

Communication Skills to deal with your customers (20%)

Mathematical Skills to do your bookkeeping, accounting, and inventory (10%)

Destination: Plant Nursery Operator

So you want to open your own plant nursery. Or maybe your ambitions are more modest and you would like to simply manage a plant nursery or sell plants that you grow on your property. Why does this career option appeal to you? It seems safe to say that you probably are famous among your friends for your green thumb. Your roses may have won prizes, or cuttings from plants in your garden may be in great demand from your neighbors. This chapter will guide you in the endeavor of turning these skills into a career by providing some preliminary information, Internet resources, and questions to ask before you traipse down this particular garden path.

The first prerequisite is that you love plants enough to make them your full time work. Whether your passion is flowers, trees, shrubs, succulents, ivy, or Venus fly traps, be certain that this is not just a passing fancy. You will be investing a lot of time, money, and effort in this endeavor. In some types of nurseries you can buy plants from wholesalers, but most nurseries grow their own stock. Until your business becomes large enough for you to hire employees, this means that you will be growing them yourself—and growing sufficient numbers of uniform plants is much different than maintaining a small, varied garden for your own pleasure. Even a modest nursery will need quite a few of each plant.

The next consideration is whether or not you are knowledgeable about horticulture. The desire to grow plants is not enough. You need to be a trained and educated expert in soil pH, fertilizers, irrigation, growing regions, plant breeding, and a host of other related skills. If you lack a formal education in horticulture, you can take some classes before you pursue your nursery dream.

To open your own nursery you will also need sound business skills. Growing plants may be a labor of love, but selling them is a job. Most nursery owners are entrepreneurs who follow procedures that apply to any small business, regardless of industry. You will have to find out who provides business licenses in your area and jump through all of the necessary hoops to get your application accepted. Depending on where you live, whether your business is home based or if you have separate premises, and whether you are in the wholesale or retail market, there are a variety of permits you will need. You will also need a business plan if you expect to get financing. If you have your own capital you will not have to account to anyone for how you spend it, but a business plan is still a wise idea. There are many books available on how to write a business plan, and no shortage of consultants who, for a fee, will help you draft one. If you do decide to hire a business consultant, look for one with experience in the plant nursery business and related industries. Check references and consider the success of businesses that have worked with the consultant.

The next step is securing business premises. If you plan to operate your nursery business out of your home, check into the zoning laws in your locality. Can you work with the restrictions that are imposed? If not, you can try requesting a variance from your town council. If you plan to lease a storefront, have your attorney look carefully at the provisions of the lease. You do not want to be on the hook for a three-year lease if your business fails in one year or, on a more optimistic note, you do not want to be tied to a small place if your business grows to the point where you need larger premises. Also consider whether the premises can meet all of the needs of an operation selling live plants, including irrigation, drainage, and compost. Is there ample parking space for customers? Is there a loading/unloading area for deliveries and pick-ups? Visit local nurseries and see how the premises are laid out. Note what they are doing well and what could be improved upon within the facilities. The more you plan ahead now, the happier you and your customers will be. If you are going to build, there is a lot of information about the design and construction process that you will need to acquire. Find contractors who have designed and built plant nurseries and greenhouses. Check their refer-

Essential Gear

Grow your business with as much skill as your seeds. If you think you can run a plant business because you can grow plants, think again. Just because your plants thrive does not mean that you will be able to pay your overheard and turn a profit. The skill set needed to run a plant business is quite different from that needed to be a good horticulturist. You need to know how to price and market your merchandise, how to keep costs down without compromising quality, and how fast to grow your business. If you grow it too fast, you could end up in debt; too slow, and you could miss opportunities. You know exactly how much food and water to give your seeds for optimum germination and your business needs the same knowledgeable care. If you are lacking in this skill set, do not despair, but do try to team up with someone who can help with the business side your nursery or hire a consultant to advise you.

ences and find out if there are any complaints against them with your local Better Business Bureau.

The next step is growing your merchandise. This can take awhile—up to a year or more in the case of trees and certain bushes. If you are growing your plants on land that you own or lease in a different location from your storefront, you will need a cost-effective method of transportation. Take fuel costs into consideration, as well as time and labor. If you want more detailed information than this chapter can provide, there are some books available on starting your own nursery business, such as Timber Press's *So You Want to Start a Nursery* by Tony Avent.

You Are Here

You can begin your journey to plant nursery management or ownership from many different locales.

Do you work in a related field? There are many possible careers in horticulture. Your transition to plant nursery owner will be easier if you already toil in one of them. If you work in landscape architecture as a landscape architect, designer, or assistant, you probably have a useful knowledge of the wholesale plant business in your region. You will have valuable insight into local demand and detailed knowledge of which plants do well in your climate. If you are a florist or floral designer you will have close ties to the wholesale flower business and a sense of local buying habits for flowers. Perhaps you have a research position in a horticultural field where you might be involved in plant breeding for the industry or for the academy. Finally, if you are not a formal member of the field of horticulture, you may own or operate a small business. If you garden in your spare time, think of putting your entrepreneurial skills to use to turn your hobby into your next business.

Do you have a business plan? Although you can start a nursery without one, having an idea of where you hope to go can help you get there. If you are reading this chapter it stands to reason that you have some interest and experience in growing plants, and you hope that your hobby can blossom into a profitable career. Making a business plan is essential if you want to secure financing for your nursery business. Investors will want to see that you are serious and know what you are doing, and that you have realistic projections for expenses and income in your first few years of operation.

Can you work part time? Nursery work is low-paying, so it may not be financially feasible for you to quit your current job to work in a nursery. If that is the case, then consider starting out working part time in the evenings or on weekends. If that is too much, see if you can downshift to part time hours at your current job. Another way to build a nursery business on a part time basis before making the leap to a full time career is to start growing and selling plants from home. Without overhead and payroll, you can grow your business at your own pace.

Navigating the Terrain

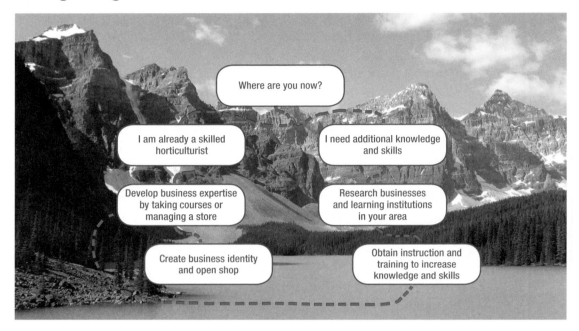

Organizing Your Expedition

Before you set out, know where you are going.

Decide on a destination. What kind of nursery would you like to own? There are four main types of nurseries: mail order, liner, wholesale, and retail.

Mail order nurseries are ideal for starting out a home-based business. Without a storefront, overhead can be kept low. On the other hand, you are limited in that what you sell must not be too fragile or perishable to ship, and the shipping costs must not be prohibitively expensive. You do not even have to grow your own plants for a mail order nursery; you can buy them wholesale. However, you must specialize in some type of plant that your customers cannot find locally. Otherwise there is no incentive for them to pay shipping costs. *Liner* nurseries grow trays of seedlings to sell to other nurseries or, less often, directly to customers. This business takes some skill in germinating seeds successfully on a grand scale and in knowing which plants will grow best where. If your seedlings do not thrive when your customers transplant them, neither will your business.

Wholesale nurseries tend to grow fewer types of plants on a larger scale. You need more land or greenhouses to operate a wholesale nursery, as well as a reliable customer base of landscapers or garden centers. What you grow will be dictated by the market in your region and the size and type of land at your disposal. With less diversity, your business is more vulnerable to problems that could wipe out single crops. *Retail* nurseries usually serve residential customers who are buying plants for their homes and gardens. Retail customers are often seeking advice, so you need to be more customer-oriented and able to teach than for other types of nurseries.

Essential Gear

Some other source of income. At the lower levels, nursery and greenhouse work is extremely low paying. The average hourly rate in 2007 was only $9.79 per hour; an average annual salary for lawn and garden store managers was $20,360. If you are planning to start your own nursery rather than seek employment at someone else's, be prepared for a long delay before you turn your first profit. Some nursery jobs come with benefits, including health and retirement savings accounts, but it is getting rarer for small businesses to be able to offer such affordable perks.

Scout the terrain. Finding a job at a local nursery is relatively easy since most of the training occurs on the job. If you have a horticulture or business-related degree or experience, you will be eligible for a higher-level job that can help you learn how to run a nursery of your own someday. If you want to open your own business straightaway, look at the local market. Which types of nurseries are thriving and expanding? Is your potential customer base mainly residential or commercial? Is there an unmet need in your area? Interview local garden clubs and landscaping businesses about their buying habits and desires. If you want to grow Christmas trees but the local Christmas tree farms are complaining that they are unable to find buyers for their stock each season, you may have to move or rethink your plans. Likewise, if you live in an ideal climate for roses but the local nurseries have limited variety and poor quality selection, you may have found your niche.

Notes from the Field

John Garfield
Plant nursery manager
Hadley, Masssachusetts

What were you doing before you decided to change careers?

I had just graduated from UMass and was working at a farm supply store selling tractors and other equipment.

Why did you change your career?

I had the chance. I didn't want to sell farm equipment indefinitely. I had done some landscaping in high school and college, and I liked working with plants. I majored in agricultural studies, with a minor in business, so I kind of had the idea of working in the farming business. I wasn't thinking nursery specifically, but I didn't have a clear idea of where I wanted to go with my degree.

Find the path that's right for you. There are a wide variety of careers in horticulture. Even if you have settled on the nursery business as the proper environment for your career to grow and thrive, you have the choice whether to work part time or full time, to run a home-based nursery business, to work in someone else's nursery, to buy an existing nursery business that is for sale, or to start your own nursery. If you start your own nursery, you have many options in terms of what types of plants you will grow, such as trees, flowers, shrubs, annuals, or perennials. You can also decide whether to operate a wholesale or retail operation, and whether to be open year-round or seasonally. You can specialize in one type of plant only, such as Christmas trees or roses, or you can operate an all-around garden center. The important consideration is that you combine what you love with what is economically viable in your area.

Go back to school. There is no specific degree required to work in a nursery or to own and operate one. Most of the necessary skills can be learned on the job, and many entrepreneurs are self-taught and naturally possess the vision and force of will to achieve their dreams. That said, there are a number of useful educational options. Both undergraduate

How did you make the transition?

You're going to laugh but my uncle owns a nursery and he offered me the job of assistant manager when it became available.

What are the keys to success in your new career?

It helps if you can deal with all kinds of people. Customers usually come in with questions, and how well you answer them, and how much they feel you are giving them personal service, is what makes them purchase from you and come back again and again. If you can earn their loyalty, you're set. We're a small nursery, but we try to provide exceptional customer service year-round. We sell Christmas trees in the winter, so the same customers that buy bulbs and fertilizer come back for their tree.

and graduate degrees in horticultural sciences provide an ideal background for the nursery business. One school with a strong horticulture program is North Caroline State University (http://www.cals.ncsu.edu/hort_sci/index.html). If your horticulture skills are strong, you may benefit from a business degree or at least some courses or seminars geared to starting and running a small business in general or a nursery business in particular. A bit of research should turn up some courses in your area. Ask local nurseries if they participate in industry seminars or continuing education. In a business degree program you may be able to take horticulture courses as electives or vice versa.

Landmarks

If you are in your twenties . . . You have a lot of options. As far as education, you can pursue horticulture and/or business-related degrees, both of which would be useful. You can get a job in a nursery and work your way up to a management position, saving money with a view towards acquiring the capital to open your own nursery someday.

If you are in your thirties or forties . . . Your options depend upon your experience. If you have horticulture experience but no capital or business acumen, you might want to get a job in a nursery to learn the business end. If you can start small by growing plants for sale on your own property, you may be able to ease into full time nursery work or upgrade gardening from a hobby to a part time business that supplements your existing income.

If you are in your fifties . . . You might be thinking of turning an erstwhile gardening hobby into a new business or you may be a horticulturist ready to branch out and start your own nursery. In either case, there are no age-related impediments to this line of work. You are not likely to face much age-related discrimination unless you grow a type of plant that requires vigorous physical labor to harvest or transplant.

If you are over sixty . . . Running a nursery could be a viable post-retirement second career. If you have money to invest in starting a nursery business, be certain that you have good business skills or seek sound advice so that you do not lose your savings.

Further Resources

American Nursery and Landscape Association   This is a membership organization that provides information on education and research. It follows legal developments related to the professions it represents and lobbies on behalf of its members. http://www.anla.org

Colorado Nursery and Greenhouse Association   This is just an example. Most states have a similar organization. Look for the one in your state. http://www.coloradonga.org/index.php?page_id=I_0

Starting a Plant Nursery or Greenhouse Business   is a useful site for neophyte nursery owners, provided by the Oregon State University Extension Service.   http://oregonstate.edu/dept/nurserystartup/new/Web_Files/labor.htm

Starting a Nursery   is much like the link above, except this site is provided by the University of Florida. http://edis.ifas.ufl.edu/TOPIC_Nursery_Startup

Dog Trainer

Dog Trainer

Career Compasses

Get your bearings on what it takes to be a successful dog trainer.

Relevant Knowledge of how to effectively and safely train dogs and, more importantly, their owners (40%)

Caring about animals is an absolute necessity. You must really love dogs (30%)

Communication Skills to impart knowledge effectively to dogs and dog owners (20%)

Ability to Manage Stress is important because your clients, both human and canine, will be difficult more often than not (10%)

Destination: Dog Trainer

So you think you are the next Dog Whisperer? If people comment on how well-behaved and obedient your dogs are, and you found the training process with your pups enjoyable and rewarding, it is a logical jump to the thought, "Hey, I could do this for a living." And, indeed, that might be possible. But before you quit your day job and print up those cute business cards with the bone-and-paw-print logo, take some time to read this chapter and find out what you need to know to launch a successful dog training business. With a little planning and foresight, it will not be such ruff-going.

Dogs have been domesticated as pets for thousands of years. They have been employed by humans for many purposes: providing security for family and possessions, guarding and herding livestock, aiding hunters in bringing in prey, providing entertainment, working in search and rescue, sniffing out explosives or drugs, assisting the disabled, and, most importantly, as loving family members—four-legged children who are no less important to their human parents than the two-legged kind. Dogs used in any of these capacities need specialized training, but by far the largest market for dog trainers is with the pet-owning public. Without proper training and guidance, the cute puppy they brought home from the shelter (one hopes) or the pet store or breeder (unfortunately, more often), is going to grow into a destructive and socially unskilled adult dog. This is true whether the pup in question is a Chihuahua or a Rottweiler.

At their worst, dogs whose training and socialization are neglected can be dangerous, putting their own lives at risk through no fault of their own in the same way that a neglected child winds up in the criminal justice system. So a dog trainer has an important role. You are the equivalent of a K–12 teacher for a human child, molding them into a productive and well-socialized adult canine citizen. Of course, you do not get to spend quite as much time with them, and you are heavily dependent upon the parents to reinforce the training on their own. It is not easy work. Loving dogs is not enough. The dogs are the easy part: It is the people who are tough to work with. In your role as trainer, you will have a brief period—perhaps only an hour a week—to work with a client's dog in person. Much of the success of your training will depend upon the willingness of the owner to do the homework you assign. Before you enter this profession you should understand that most owners will not do much. They will come to you after problems have started—i.e., long after they should have begun training—and they will expect you to fix the problem with no effort on their part.

Now you understand some of the challenges of this job. Let us consider a few more. What kind of experience do you have handling dogs? If you are a vet tech, groomer, dog walker, or otherwise involved in handling a variety of types of dogs, great—you have an advantage. If your only experience is training, showing, or otherwise handling your own dogs or a particular breed of dogs, you will need to augment your experience before you can launch your own business. The principles that underpin your training and the exercises that you will use in the process will not vary much from dog to dog. But each dog is an individual and each breed has certain traits that are stronger than others.

Each trainer is different. Some use clickers or other aids and gimmicks. Most trainers today use positive reinforcement methods. If you are thinking of training professionally, you have probably already started along the road of codifying a way of training that has worked for you. In order to reach more clients than live in their local areas, some trainers publish dog-training books. Other trainers run camps or clinics for dogs and their owners. It is certainly not true that you cannot teach an old dog new tricks (you should know that already if you are considering dog training as a career), but some trainers do specialize in puppy training. A dog trainer's area of specialization can be borne of his or her personal experience. Pamela Dennison, for example, specializes in working with aggression issues because of her experience successfully rehabilitating a border collie, Shadow, whose success story she chronicles in her book *Bringing Light to Shadow*.

Essential Gear

Publish your training philosophy. Trends in dog training change continually, just like in other fields, but certain distinctions in core philosophies remain. There has been a gradual shift from negative-reinforcement methods to positive ones, but not all trainers are on-board. You should post your training philosophy on a Web site and direct prospective clients to it before they make a decision. You can also print handouts to give out to clients, and, ultimately, publish your own books on the subject.

Ah, the wheels are really turning now. What can you bring to this profession that is unique? Perhaps you or someone you know has a service dog and you have been inspired to train these specialized canine helpers. As acceptance of service dogs increases, and their use spreads to more types of disabilities, the need for trainers is expected to rise. The use of dogs in search-and-rescue and forensic work is also on the increase. Getting a job training dogs outside of the pet market is not easy—you will need some specialized training yourself, and you will need to live in an area with a facility that conducts such training—but your chances of full time employment are slightly higher if you can land one of these jobs. If you are not looking for full time employment, you will have an easier time in this highly competitive field.

There are a variety of working environment options for dog trainers. Some are employed by stores like Petco to run in-house training classes. Successful dog trainers can sometimes open their own facility where clients come for classes and to use particular equipment, such as an agility course. These trainers often employ other trainers to run some of their classes. If you have your own facilities, you have the option of working with more than one dog at a time in a classroom environment. Most trainers offer one-on-one consultations at clients' houses. This is more common for behavioral issues than for basic puppy training. It helps to meet the dog in its home and to tailor the training to the dog's particular issues and circumstances. Whether you are working full time or training outside the demands of another job, know that many clients will expect you to be available on evenings or weekends when they are home from their work. A certain amount of flexibility about working hours is important for establishing yourself in this field, but this can also be seen as an advantage as you unmoor from your previous job and chart your course to becoming a dog trainer.

You Are Here

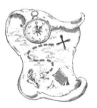

You can begin your journey to dog training from many different locales.

Do you work in a related field? Anyone who has a dog is in need of the services of a competent dog trainer, whether they know it or not. And people involved with animals to any degree have a tendency to have dogs, and know people with more dogs. If you work with animals in any capacity in your current profession, you probably have a network of acquaintances that can serve as a potential client base. If you work with horses, for example, you have probably noticed that horse people tend to have dogs. Perhaps you work in a pet supplies store, where dozens of people with dogs walk through the door each day. If you work in a vet's office or in a boarding or grooming facility or animal shelter, you have a tremendous advantage in segueing into your new profession. If you are employed in law enforcement or the military, you might be able to request a transfer to a unit that trains dogs. Do you show your dogs or compete in obedience or agility? Perhaps you pursue dog-related sports like sledding or herding? Again, these events, and their associated membership organizations and online groups, are ideal places to connect with potential clients. If you do not have these connections, do not despair, but do see how you might get involved in activities or jobs that would enable you to meet potential clients.

Do you have an animal-related degree? There is no degree offered in dog-training, and no nationally recognized certification or licensing program, but a degree in animal behavioral sciences or a related field might lend you some credibility in the crucial early phase of building a client base. Once you have established a network of satisfied clients, business will come by word of mouth, and a degree will not matter as much.

Essential Gear

Pack your steamer trunk with business cards and advertise. The key to getting any kind of freelance work, whether you are a dog trainer or a carpenter, is networking. Someone who has seen you and your dogs at shows or rallies, or someone who has seen other dogs that you have trained, is more likely to hire you to train his or her dogs than a stranger. Pass out your business cards to local canine businesses—vet's offices, groomers, pet supplies stores (NOT stores that sell dogs), rescues and shelters, are all good places to advertise. Word of mouth and reputation will help you, and so will business cards with a memorable canine-themed logo and a sophisticated Web site.

Can you work part time? Building up a steady flow of clients barking at your front door is going to take some time. How are you going to support yourself until your business supports you? If you can retain your current job, and begin by training in the evenings and on weekends, you may find the financial transition smoother. If your current job has flexible hours or the option of telecommuting, even better. You will find that being available at times convenient for your potential clients is crucial for gaining business.

Navigating the Terrain

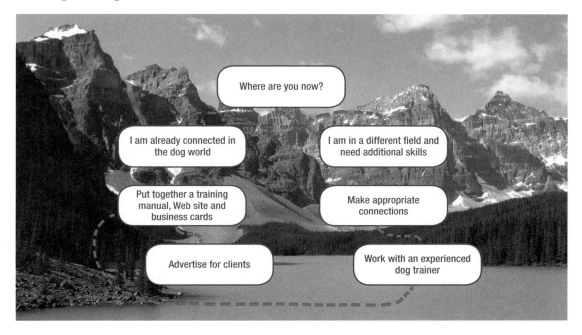

Organizing Your Expedition

Before you set out, know where you are going.

Decide on a destination. What kind of dog trainer would you like to be? Not all dog trainers work with pet dogs. Some train dogs for law enforcement and the military, or various types of security work. This field includes bomb- and drug-sniffing dogs, as well as dogs who work in rescue and recovery missions. There is also a need for trainers of service dogs. These dogs are employed by hearing, sight, or mobility-impaired individuals to enable them to live more independently. Increasingly, service dogs are working for people whose disabilities are hidden, such as sufferers of epilepsy or diabetes, because certain dogs have an ability to detect seizures or other health emergencies that can occur with these conditions. Dogs employed in the entertainment industry also need special training,

Notes from the Field

Pam Dennison
Dog trainer
Founder, Positive Motivation Dog Training, LLC
Belvidere, New Jersey

What were you doing before you decided to change careers?
I was a printing estimator/sales/purchasing agent.

Why did you change your career?
The printing industry died in the late 1980s, so I really had no choice. I had been involved with competitive obedience and agility with my border collies, and I was interested in developing my passion for these disciplines, and my love for dogs, into a business.

How did you make the transition?
I bought a grooming business and worked part time in the printing industry, then quit the printing job and did grooming part time and started training part time. Not too long after that, I decided that I hated grooming, sold the shop and went full time training. Then I added writing books on dog training as part of my income.

whether they are actors in television or film or employed in live entertainment shows. Trainers can also specialize in preparing dogs for the show ring, or specialized activities like agility or competitive obedience. These are some of the options that might appeal to you besides being a pet dog trainer.

Scout the terrain. If you plan to become a pet dog trainer, start by joining the Association of Pet Dog Trainers. Avail yourself of the resources on their Web site, and look at the Web sites of individual trainers. Reading books written by dog trainers will help you get started and begin to define your training philosophy and methodology, but there is no substitute for experience. Utilize your connections to assess the dog training possibilities in your area. Are they large pet supply stores that have trainers on staff? Are there doggy day care facilities that offer training classes? Do you live near a facility that trains service dogs? Do you have

What are the keys to success in your new career?

Diversify! In addition to regular training classes, from puppy kindergarten to advanced beginners, I offer classes leading to the CGC (Canine Good Citizen) and TDI (Therapy Dog) testing, most forms of competition (obedience, rally, agility), and private and group classes for dogs with problem behaviors, including aggression. I have added specialty classes to my schedule, including Loose Leash Walking, The Multiple Dog Household, Kid Proof Your Dog and Dog Proof Your Kid, Everybody in the Pool (where your dog learns to swim in three different water sources—a river, a lake and a pool), Acting Classes for Dogs (where your dog learns behaviors needed for print ads, commercials, TV shows and movies), several summer camp programs for different behavior issues, and a variety of other classes as demand warrants. I also present at seminars and canine events, in addition to writing books and making DVDs. Although it is important to diversify, you also need to develop a niche. Because of my experience with my aggressive border collie, Shadow, which led to my first book, Bringing Light to Shadow, I have found a niche in training aggressive dogs. Many of my books, DVDs, lectures, appearances in various media, specialty classes, and camps deal with aggressive dogs. Developing my people skills has also been an important part of achieving success in this field.

relationships with vets or groomers where you could leave your business cards? A little sniffing around will help you determine the possibilities for making a living in your new field in your area.

Find the path that's right for you. Consider, above all, your financial situation. A dog trainer is usually a freelance consultant, an independent contractor who usually has no guarantee of another dog to train when the current one trots out the door. You may need to juggle marketing yourself with doing the actual training, which can be a difficult balance to strike on your own. You will be unlikely to have benefits or paid vacation time, and scheduling training to suit your clients' schedules will be paramount for building a good reputation in the business. Do you need health insurance? Can you afford to live on part time wages while you are starting out and building your client base? The answers to these questions will help you set out on the right path.

Go back to school. As noted above, there are no particular degree or certification requirements for dog trainers. You are unlikely to have to go back to school to enter this field; however, you do need considerable experience working with all kinds of dogs, with a variety of behavioral issues. Although you may not need to attend classes, you may need to work with dogs in some capacity, or assist a more experienced trainer, before striking out on your own. If you decide that you want to train dogs for the military or law enforcement, you may need to join one of these professions, and complete a general training program before you can specialize in a canine unit. These organizations, as well as specialized facilities that train service dogs for the handicapped, may have their own degree requirements.

Landmarks

If you are in your twenties . . . You may be unhappy in your first job and find yourself searching for a career that you can really sink your teeth into. If you love dogs, and have experience handling them, then you have a lot of options for moving into dog training full time. If you are still in school, you can major in animal behavior. Even if you are out of school, you may be living at home or have the flexibility to live with roommates, both options that will enable you to accept a lower salary as you build up clientele. This is also a great age to get an entry-level job in a related field, such as in a vet hospital or at a dog groomer. You could also get a job as a handler of show dogs and build your reputation in the ring. Dog trainers are not likely to face much age discrimination. A twentysomething trainer may have worked with dogs all his or her life and be extremely competent even at a young age. The energy you have at this age will also come in handy.

If you are in your thirties or forties . . . Then you have probably given a lot of thought to changing into this career. Perhaps you already work with dogs and have found that you have a knack for training. Your biggest obstacle may be finding a way to make this career transition work financially. You might find that you can develop dog training as a sideline occupation at first. You may not be able to train full time, but part time experience can help you set sail toward a career change on the horizon.

If you are in your fifties . . . You can probably relate to the advice for younger career changers, above. The issue with changing into a career that relies on reputation, work of mouth, and self-marketing, is ensuring that your income consistently covers your expenses. If you really want to be a dog trainer, consider how you might be able to downsize your life and cut expenses to make it work.

If you are over sixty . . . You may have the means to take up dog training and see how it goes. If you are retired, then some of the pressure may be off of you to make a living from training. You might be able to afford to train at discounted rates or on a volunteer basis at first to help you establish your reputation. You might start by training dogs for the poor or giving educational classes about safe dog handling to children in schools. The benefits of animal companions for seniors are well known now. If you live in or near a retirement community, you might consider specializing in training dogs for the elderly.

Further Resources

Association of Pet Dog Trainers The main professional membership organization for dog trainers. It provides education in positive reinforcement-based training and networking for members, and its membership listing provides a resource for the public in choosing a trainer in their area. The $150 annual membership fee is a worthwhile investment in your career. http://www.apdt.com

Dogwise.com An online store of dog-related literature and selected products. It has a large variety of dog training books, including many that are essential for a career in dog training. Browse the "For the Professional Dog Trainer" section. http://www.dogwise.com

Clicker Training A popular fad in animal (not just dog) training today. Whether or not you choose to use clickers in your own training, you must at least be conversant with the method. http://www.clickertraining.com

Dr. P's Dog Training Library An incredibly extensive online database of dog-related information. If you are looking for it, it's probably here. http://www.uwsp.edu/psych/dog/library.htm

Horticulturist/ Garden Designer

Horticulturist/ Garden Designer

Career Compasses

Get your bearings on what it takes to be a successful horticulturist/garden fesigner.

Relevant Knowledge of plants and their characteristics (40%)

Caring about the environment is an absolute necessity. You must be committed to sustainable design and the maintenance of healthy, native ecosystems (30%)

Communication Skills to get a clear sense of your clients' needs and preferences (20%)

Mathematical Skills for measuring and drawing designs, and for a variety of scientific work conducted by plant breeders and other highly technical areas of specialization within the field (10%)

Destination: Horticulturist/Garden Designer

You really like plants. Let us start with that as the common characteristic that defines everyone reading this chapter. Beyond that feature, it grows more difficult to pinpoint what you have in common because horticulture is such a broad field, encompassing everyone from a garden designer in a historic village museum who re-creates historically accurate kitchen and flower gardens, to a genetic engineer working on designing new pesticide-resistant species of corn or soy for Monsanto, to a landscape architect planning the landscaping that will be installed around the community pool in a new suburban housing development. All of these disparate professions are related to horticulture, but the jobs are really quite different. This fact presents opportunities as well as challenges, both in terms of making choices and in obtaining new and sometimes highly technical qualifications. But do not fret; this chapter will guide you on a clear path through the corn maze of options and qualifications. Let us start by putting some possible employment options under the microscope.

Essential Gear

Encyclopedic knowledge of plant taxonomy. The scientific classification of plants involves grouping each plant in a hierarchy that consists of kingdom, phylum, class, order, family, genus, and species. This system allows newly created or discovered plants to be easily catalogued and identified. Horticulturalists are expected to be intimately familiar with botanical nomenclature, and able to shift comfortably between using scientific terminology with peers and common plant names with clients and other laypeople.

If you think about it logically, any human-made green space has to first be designed and planned, then planted, and then maintained. Horticulturists are involved in all of these stages.

The first stage, design, features the work of a landscape designer. A designer in any field is an artist of sorts. He or she needs to have an ability to see things that do not yet exist in reality so as to formulate a vision for what an object or a space should look like. A landscape designer's canvas is a plain patch of dirt, and his or her palette consists of colors found in trees, shrubs, flowers, and other plants. This vision needs to take into account many technical and site-specific factors, such as sunlight, rainfall, soil pH, the proposed use of the space by humans, the amount of maintenance the owners of the space are willing or able to undertake, and the species of wildlife that are considered desirable or undesirable to attract to the space. The space is likely to include not just plants, but water and water features, walls, fences, paths, pools or sporting areas, or even resident animals. Color and beauty throughout the year is usually a goal for most projects. Landscape architects sometimes work with landscape assistants who are students of landscape design or experienced gardeners without a formal landscaping-related degree. Working as an assistant to an established designer can be a useful way to learn the business and make connections to facilitate your career change, as well as gain valuable practical experience while you are in school.

Another type of horticulturist who must have visual artistic talent and a flair for attractive and appropriate visual design is a florist. Florists often work with flowers and other foliage that has been cut from the soil, and they must know how to preserve their bloom for as long as the occasion demands. Florists must be able to match flowers with the clothing and décor of various settings, especially weddings, holidays, and other formal and festive occasions when clients are likely to splurge on their services. Florists must know the 'language of flowers,' an old-fashioned system of pairing certain types or colors of flowers with various sentiments and rites of passage. They must also be intimately familiar with the properties of their delicate wares, such as their scent and their propensity to shed pollen. Business management acumen is an additional skill set that is useful for florists who own or manage their own shops.

Nursery workers are covered in a separate chapter but it is worth mentioning that they work in the branch of horticulture that supplies the raw materials to both landscape designers and florists. These horticulturalists work in wholesale and retail garden centers. They buy plants, choose what stock the nursery will carry, and oversee the growing process. Trained horticulturists are sometimes managers or owners of there retail plant outlets. Organic farming is another related field that is also covered in its own chapter in this volume. One employment option that you might not think of at first is working as a horticultural therapist. The therapeutic power of animals and music and even color and scent is well known, and there are specialist therapists in each of these areas. Working with plants has also proven to be therapeutic, as any gardener knows, and horticultural therapists work with children and adults with emotional problems and physical disabilities, including senior citizens and autistic children.

Once the designers have laid the groundwork, so to speak, another category of horticulturists steps in to maintain their work. Groundskeepers, gardeners, and related workers like arborists see that the landscape planned by the designer remains healthy and alive. Golf course managers, park superintendents, and irrigation specialists are examples of some highly specialized professions in the area of horticultural maintenance.

An entirely different branch of horticulture is tied to agricultural productivity. Workers in this specialty spend more time in a laboratories than in gardens, conducting experiments that have the goal of improving the appearance, hardiness, and transportability of produce, as well as the yield of crops, their flavor, nutritional content, and resistance to pesticides. These plant physiologists, plant pathologists, and biochemists usually work for large agribusiness conglomerates or at academic institutions with strong research programs in plant sciences that are sponsored by both the government and the private sector. A strong science background rather than an affinity for visual design is the prerequisite for this end of the horticulture career spectrum. The biotech industry is growing and branching worldwide, and there are currently more jobs than trained workers in this field in the United States. Jobs in this area can pay in the six-figure range, easily double what most landscape designers and florists make. However, the educational requirements are more rigorous, with a Ph.D. a necessary prerequisite to most academic jobs and most biotech ones as well.

You Are Here

You can begin your journey to a career in horticulture from many different locales.

Do you work in a related field? Horticulture is such a broad field that there are many other career paths that are tangentially related. Landscape design is in the same family as architectural design, and plant breeding and genetic engineering are linked with other careers in scientific research. Farming and working in a nursery or greenhouse also leap to mind as related careers. Most any job that involves working outdoors or with plants, such as forester or environmental educator, could be construed as related. The value in working in a related field is that it makes the transition to a horticultural career easier. You may have a better idea of where, in the broad field of horticulture, your talents, interests, and skills will best fit.

Do you have a horticulture-related degree? Any degree in the hard sciences, but especially plant biology, botany, organic chemistry, agricultural sciences, and even genetic engineering or mathematics are all good launching pads for a career in horticulture. A degree in business management can be helpful if your aim is to manage a greenhouse. Landscape design has quite specific degree requirements so you are unlikely to already have a degree in landscape architecture if you are just now considering changing careers into this field.

Can you work part time? Because of its rather stringent and specific degree requirements, a career change into the field of horticulture is likely to require a return to school. Transplanting yourself from your current career and establishing strong roots in the soil of your new field might be best accomplished by reducing your hours at your current job whilst you pursue a new degree, or else obtaining a part time position in your new field, such as nursery worker or landscape assistant, that is at a lower level than the one you eventually hope to acquire upon completion of your education. The more flexibility you have with your work routine, the smoother the transition to your new career environment will be.

Navigating the Terrain

Where are you now?

I have a related degree and experience

I am in a different field altogether

Put together a résumé

Identify your particular interests and research schools

Apply for jobs

Go back to school for a horticulture degree

Stories from the Field

Frederick Law Olmsted
Landscape designer
New York, New York

If you ever wonder if you can rise to the loftiest heights of a new career coming from a completely different field, consider the biography of Frederick Law Olmsted. Olmsted is best known as the designer of Central Park, but the National Park Service has dubbed him, "the founder of American landscape architecture and the nation's foremost parkmaker." Olmsted received a lucky start in life, being born into a well-off merchant's family in Connecticut. Poor eyesight caused him to abandon plans to attend Yale College, and he instead found work as first a seaman and then a merchant before settling into a career in journalism. He was commissioned by a New York newspaper to write some investigative articles on slavery, which helped to raise abolitionist sentiments in New England. Olmsted was also the cofounder of *The Nation* magazine. His parents had nurtured an interest in nature in their children, and Olmsted took a trip to England to study and write about its public parks. He was friends with Andrew Jackson Downing, editor of *The Horticulturist* magazine, who proposed the development of

Organizing Your Expedition

Before you set out, know where you are going.

Decide on a destination. There are many different specialty areas in the field of horticulture, each with its own career possibilities. Some possible specialties include pomology (fruit production), olericulture (vegetable production), floriculture (flower production), nursery crop production, and landscape design, which can include both commercial and residential landscaping. The American Society for Horticultural Science (ASHS) Web site has a section on career possibilities that features over 50 horticulturalists in various specialties describing what they do through text, photos, and audio and video recordings. You might enjoy perusing this resource even if you have already picked an area of concentration.

a central park for New York. After Downing was tragically killed in a steamboat explosion, Olmsted and Calvert Vaux together entered the design contest for the new park, and won.

In 1857, Olmsted was appointed superintendent of Central Park. This was during the park's early design phase, which enabled Olmsted to plan the entire 843-acre park to their specifications. The diversity of the landscape in Central Park is remarkable for providing a feeling of openness and serenity in the middle of Manhattan. Many hills, winding paths and a wide variety of paths, bridges, playing fields and water features give the park diversity and interest. Olmsted stayed on to oversee the early development of the park, and he and Vaux went on to design other famous parks, including Prospect Park in Brooklyn, and municipal parks in Buffalo, Louisville, and other cities, along with the nation's oldest state park at Niagara Falls, New York. Among many notable commissions, Olmsted was invited to redesign and U.S. Capitol grounds, as well as the 1893 Chicago World's Fair Midway Plaisance, and the grounds of the Biltmore estate. After Olmsted opened his own firm in 1883 in Brookline, Massachusetts, he designed Boston's well-known "Emerald Necklace" of open spaces around the city. His two sons took over his firm upon his retirement in 1895. His family estate is now a national historic landmark.

The work environment in various jobs will differ. Some horticulturists work in a traditional greenhouse or a hydroponic growing facility. Landscape designers may spend a fair portion of their work day sitting at a computer or drafting table in a landscape design or architectural firm, but they will also work on site at locations that can range from pubic parks, monuments, and gardens to private estates and commercial properties. Some landscape designers have the luxury of specializing in residential or commercial work, but other may need to take many types of jobs to make ends meet.

Scout the terrain. Not all horticulture career options are available in all locales. Certain types of research into plant breeding and agrochemicals are associated with research universities and the laboratories of international agribusiness like Monsanto. Consider if you are willing to relocate for your job of choice. Opportunities in landscape design exist throughout the country, of course. There are not large areas that are completely paved over—yet. But the demands of the job and required expertise are strongly localized. Landscape design skills are not easily transferable between desert, coastal, inland, and northern climates because of the knowledge of native species, soil, irrigation, and other information that is climate-specific.

Essential Gear

A strong moral compass. This is not human or veterinary medicine or another field where tough moral choices are known to go with the territory. But, actually, it is similar. Genetic engineering of plants is a large and growing area of employment in this field. Creating new species of plants and releasing them into the wild has moral implications because of the potentially destructive effects new species can have on habitats. Creating seeds that are resistant to agrochemicals creates the potential for more such chemicals to be used. Even more morally questionable is the creation of sterile seeds that require farmers to purchase new ones from the manufacturer each year. Landscape designers are not immune from moral dilemmas either as they must decide whether to use non-native species in their designs, and whether to incorporate existing plants that may have historic value or play a major part in the local ecosystem.

Find the path that's right for you. You know you love plants and you have decided that you want a career that involves digging in the dirt and watching green shoots grow, but the many employment options in the field of horticulture can seem bewildering. Before you commit to an expensive course of study that might lead to a less than ideal job, find out all you can about the specialty that you are considering. Most crucially, talk to people in the field. There is a world of difference between a residential landscape designer and a scientist who breeds sterile and pesticide resistant seeds for Monsanto. Although both jobs fall broadly under the field of horticulture, it is unlikely that they could both appeal to any one person.

Go back to school. Most horticulture jobs will require at least an undergraduate degree, usually a bachelor of science in one of the hard sciences such as plant biology, organic chemistry, or agricultural science. Mathematics courses are a desirable addition for many fields as well. A few lower level jobs, such as gardener, may accept a two-year associate's degree coupled with on-the-job experience and extensive plant knowledge, but advancement is likely to be impossible without the requisite advanced degree. Most horticultural careers require a master's degree and many call for a doctoral degree.

Landmarks

If you are in your twenties . . . If you are still in school, spend your school holidays working in nurseries and greenhouses, or even at flower shops and landscape design firms. Also investigate co-op programs and internship opportunities available through your school. Contact businesses where you would like to work and ask if you can conduct an informational interview to find out what you need to do to get hired. Ascertain if job prospects in your area are good for when you plan to graduate, and find out what additional education is required for your chosen horticultural specialty.

If you are in your thirties or forties . . . Consider if it is feasible for you to return to school full time for a degree in landscape design. See if it is possible for you to take related science courses, such as botany, biology, and chemistry, at a local university part time, structured around your current employment. If you already have a B.S. in a science-related field, look into master's programs in your preferred specialty area.

If you are in your fifties . . . A lot depends upon how closely related your existing degree and job experience is to your new career choice. If they are far removed from one another, you need to be prepared to go back to school, possibly at the undergraduate level at first. Nontraditional students are becoming more common, so the only issue is whether you have the means to attend full time. See if your employer provides tuition reimbursement or a flexible schedule.

If you are over sixty . . . The advice for those in their fifties applies to you as well. If you are retired, finding time to return to full time education might not pose a problem for you, but keep in mind that pursuit of a doctoral degree will keep you in school for many years even if you are able to attend a program full time.

Further Resources

GardenWeb A comprehensive site that provides information on many types of plants. It is an invaluable resource for garden design. http://www.gardenweb.com

Gardening Launch Pad Provides links to online gardening resources. http://gardeninglaunchpad.com

National Biological Information Infrastructure (NBII) Contains links to articles on botany. The NBII Program is administered by the Biological Informatics Office of the U.S. Geological Survey. http://www.nbii.gov/portal/community/Communities/Plants,_Animals_&_Other_Organisms/Botany

The Garden Helper Provides gardening advice for both beginning and experienced gardeners. http://www.thegardenhelper.com

Appendix A

Going Solo: Starting Your Own Business

Starting your own business can be very rewarding—not only in terms of potential financial success, but also in the pleasure derived from building something from the ground up, contributing to the community, being your own boss, and feeling reasonably in control of your fate. However, business ownership carries its own obligations—both in terms of long hours of hard work and new financial and legal responsibilities. If you succeed in growing your business, your responsibilities only increase. Many new business owners come in expecting freedom only to find themselves chained tighter to their desks than ever before. Still, many business owners find greater satisfaction in their career paths than do workers employed by others.

The Internet has also changed the playing field for small business owners, making it easier than ever before to strike out on your own. While small mom-and-pop businesses such as hairdressers and grocery stores have always been part of the economic landscape, the Internet has made reaching and marketing to a niche easier and more profitable. This has made possible a boom in *microbusinesses*. Generally, a microbusiness is considered to have under ten employees. A microbusiness is also sometimes called a *SoHo* for "small office/home office."

The following appendix is intended to explain, in general terms, the steps in launching a small business, no matter whether it is selling your Web-design services or opening a pizzeria with business partners. It will also point out some of the things you will need to bear in mind. Remember also that the particular obligations of your municipality, state, province, or country may vary, and that this is by no means a substitute for doing your own legwork. Further suggested reading is listed at the end.

Crafting a Business Plan

It has often been said that success is 1 percent inspiration and 99 percent perspiration. However, the interface between the two can often be hard to achieve. The first step to taking your idea and making it reality is constructing a viable *business plan*. The purpose of a business plan is to think things all the way through, to make sure your ideas really are profitable, and to figure out the "who, what, when, where, why, and how" of your business. It fills in the details for three areas: your goals, why you think they are attainable, and how you plan to get to there. "You need to know where you're going before you take that first step," says Drew Curtis, successful Internet entrepreneur and founder of the popular newsfilter Fark.com.

Take care in writing your business plan. Generally, these documents contain several parts: An *executive summary* stating the essence of the plan; a *market summary* explaining how a need exists for the product and service you will supply and giving an idea of potential profitability by comparing your business to similar organizations; a *company description* which includes your products and services, why you think your organization will succeed, and any special advantages you have, as well as a description of *organization* and *management*; and your *marketing and sales strategy*. This last item should include market highlights and demographic information and trends that relate to your proposal. Also include a *funding request* for the amount of start-up capital you will need. This is supported by a section on *financials*, or the sort of cash flow you can expect, based on market analysis, projection, and comparison with existing companies. Other needed information, such as personal financial history, résumés, legal documents, or pictures of your product, can be placed in *appendices*.

Use your business plan to get an idea of how much startup money is necessary and to discipline your thinking and challenge your preconceived notions before you develop your cash flow. The business plan will tell you how long it will take before you turn a profit, which in turn is linked to how long it will before you will be able to pay back investors or a bank loan—which is something that anyone supplying you with money will want to know. Even if you are planning to subside on grants or you are not planning on investment or even starting a for-profit company, the discipline imposed by the business plan is still the first step to organizing your venture.

A business plan also gives you a realistic view of your personal financial obligations. How long can you afford to live without regular income? How are you going to afford medical insurance? When will your business begin turning a profit? How much of a profit? Will you need to reinvest your profits in the business, or can you begin living off of them? Proper planning is key to success in any venture.

A final note on business plans: Take into account realistic expected profit minus realistic costs. Many small business owners begin by underestimating start-ups and variable costs (such as electricity bills), and then underpricing their product. This effectively paints them into a corner from which it is hard to make a profit. Allow for realistic market conditions on both the supply and the demand side.

Partnering Up

You should think long and hard about the decision to go into business with a partner (or partners). Whereas other people can bring needed capital, expertise, and labor to a business, they can also be liabilities. The questions you need to ask yourself are:

☞ Will this person be a full and equal partner? In other words, are they able to carry their own weight? Make a full and fair assessment of your potential partner's personality. Going into business with someone who lacks a work ethic, or prefers giving directions to working in the trenches, can be a frustrating experience.

☞ What will they contribute to the business? For instance, a partner may bring in start-up money, facilities, or equipment. However, consider if this is enough of a reason to bring them on board. You may be able to get the same advantages in another way—for instance, renting a garage rather than working out of your partner's. Likewise, doubling skill sets does not always double productivity.

☞ Do they have any liabilities? For instance, if your prospective partner has declared bankruptcy in the past, this can hurt your collective venture's ability to get credit.

☞ Will the profits be able to sustain all the partners? Many start-up ventures do not turn profits immediately, and what little they do produce can be spread thin amongst many partners. Carefully work out the math.

Also bear in mind that going into business together can put a strain on even the best personal relationships. No matter whether it is family, friends, or strangers, keep everything very professional with written agreements regarding these investments. Get everything in writing, and be clear where obligations begin and end. "It's important to go into business with the right people," says Curtis. "If you don't—if it degrades into infighting and petty bickering—it can really go south quickly."

Incorporating. . . or Not

Think long and hard about incorporating. Starting a business often requires a fairly large—and risky—financial investment, which in turn exposes you to personal liability. Furthermore, as your business grows, so does your risk. Incorporating can help you shield yourself from this liability. However, it also has disadvantages.

To begin with, incorporating is not necessary for conducting professional transactions such as obtaining bank accounts and credit. You can do this as a sole proprietor, partnership, or simply by filing a DBA ("doing business as") statement with your local court (also known as "trading as" or an "assumed business name"). The DBA is an accounting entity that facilitates commerce and keeps your business' money separate from your own. However, the DBA does not shield you from responsibility if your business fails. It is entirely possible to ruin your credit, lose your house, and have your other assets seized in the unfortunate event of bankruptcy.

The purpose of incorporating is to shield yourself from personal financial liability. In case the worst happens, only the business' assets can be taken. However, this is not always the best solution. Check your local laws: Many states have laws that prevent a creditor from seizing a non-incorporated small business' assets in case of owner bankruptcy. If you are a corporation, however, the things you use to do business that are owned by the corporation—your office equipment, computers, restaurant refrigerators, and other essential equipment—may be seized by creditors, leaving you no way to work yourself out of debt. This is why it is imperative to consult with a lawyer.

There are other areas in which being a corporation can be an advantage, such as business insurance. Depending on your business needs, insurance can be for a variety of things: malpractice, against delivery failures or spoilage, or liability against defective products or accidents. Furthermore, it is easier to hire employees, obtain credit, and buy health insurance as an organization than as an individual. However, on the downside, corporations are subject to specific and strict laws concerning management and ownership. Again, you should consult with a knowledgeable legal expert.

Among the things you should discuss with your legal expert are the advantages and disadvantages of incorporating in your jurisdiction and which type of incorporation is best for you. The laws on liability and how much of your profit will be taken away in taxes vary widely by state and country. Generally, most small businesses owners opt for *limited liability companies* (LLCs), which gives them more control and a more flexible management structure. (Another possibility is a *limited liability partnership*, or *LLP*, which is especially useful for professionals such as doctors and lawyers.) Finally, there is the *corporation*, which is characterized by transferable ownerships shares, perpetual succession, and, of course, limited liability.

Most small businesses are sole proprietorships, partnerships, or privately-owned corporations. In the past, not many incorporated, since it was necessary to have multiple owners to start a corporation. However, this is changing, since it is now possible in many states for an individual to form a corporation. Note also that the form your business takes is usually not set in stone: A sole proprietorship or partnership can switch to become an LLC as it grows and the risks increase; furthermore, a successful LLC can raise capital by changing its structure to become a corporation and selling stock.

Legal Issues

Many other legal issues besides incorporating (or not) need to be addressed before you start your business. It is impossible to speak directly to every possible business need in this brief appendix, since regulations, licenses, and health and safety codes vary by industry and locality. A restaurant in Manhattan, for instance, has to deal not only with the usual issues such as health inspectors, the state liquor board, but obscure regulations such as New York City's cabaret laws, which prohibit dancing without a license in a place where alcohol is sold. An asbestos-abatement company, on the other hand, has a very different set of standards it has to abide by, including federal regulations. Researching applicable laws is part of starting up any business.

Part of being a wise business owner is knowing when you need help. There is software available for things like bookkeeping, business plans, and Web site creation, but generally, consulting with a knowledgeable professional—an accountant or a lawyer (or both)—is the smartest move. One of the most common mistakes is believing that just because you have expertise in the technical aspects of a certain field, you know all about running a business in that field. Whereas some people may balk at the expense, by suggesting the best way to deal with possible problems, as well as cutting through red tape and seeing possible pitfalls that you may not even have been aware of, such professionals usually more than make up for their cost. After all, they have far more experience at this than does a first-time business owner!

Financial

Another necessary first step in starting a business is obtaining a bank account. However, having the account is not as important as what you do with it. One of the most common problems with small businesses is undercapitalization—especially in brick-and-mortar businesses that sell or make something, rather than service-based businesses. The rule of thumb is that you should have access to money equal to your first year's anticipated profits, plus start-up expenses. (Note that this is not the same as having the money on hand—see the discussion on lines of credit, below.) For instance, if your annual rent, salaries, and equipment will cost $50,000 and you expect $25,000 worth of profit in your first year, you should have access to $75,000 worth of financing.

You need to decide what sort of financing you will need. Small business loans have both advantages and disadvantages. They can provide critical start-up credit, but in order to obtain one, your personal credit will need to be good, and you will, of course, have to pay them off with interest. In general, the more you and your partners put into the business yourselves, the more credit lenders will be willing to extend to you.

Equity can come from your own personal investment, either in cash or an equity loan on your home. You may also want to consider bringing on partners—at least limited financial partners—as a way to cover start-up costs.

It is also worth considering obtaining a line of credit instead of a loan. A loan is taken out all at once, but with a line of credit, you draw on the money as you need it. This both saves you interest payments and means that you have the money you need when you need it. Taking out too large of a loan can be worse than having no money at all! It just sits there collecting interest—or, worse, is spent on something utterly unnecessary—and then is not around when you need it most.

The first five years are the hardest for any business venture; your venture has about double the usual chance of closing in this time (1 out of 6, rather than 1 out of 12). You will probably have to tighten your belt at home, as well as work long hours and keep careful track of your business expenses. Be careful with your money. Do not take unnecessary risks, play it conservatively, and always keep some capital in reserve for emergencies. The hardest part of a new business, of course, is the learning curve of figuring out what, exactly, you need to do to make a profit, and so the best advice is to have plenty of savings—or a job to provide income—while you learn the ropes.

One thing you should not do is count on venture capitalists or "angel investors," that is, businesspeople who make a living investing on other businesses in the hopes that their equity in the company will increase in value. Venture capitalists have gotten something of a reputation as indiscriminate spendthrifts due to some poor choices made during the dot-com boom of the late 1990s, but the fact is that most do not take risks on unproven products. Rather, they are attracted to young companies that have the potential to become regional or national powerhouses and give better-than-average returns. Nor are venture capitalists are endless sources of money; rather, they are savvy businesspeople who are usually attracted to companies that have already experienced a measure of success. Therefore, it is better to rely on your own resources until you have proven your business will work.

Bookkeeping 101

The principles of double-entry bookkeeping have not changed much since its invention in the fifteenth century: one column records debits, and one records credits. The trick is *doing* it. As a small business owner, you need to be disciplined and meticulous at recording your finances. Thankfully, today there is software available that can do everything from tracking payables and receivables to running checks and generating reports.

Honestly ask yourself if you are the sort of person who does a good job keeping track of finances. If you are not, outsource to a bookkeeping company or hire someone to come in once or twice a week to enter invoices and generate checks for you. Also remember that if you have employees or even freelancers, you will have to file tax forms for them at the end of the year.

Another good idea is to have an accountant for your business to handle advice and taxes (federal, state, local, sales tax, etc.). In fact, consulting with an a certified public accountant is a good idea in general, since they are usually aware of laws and rules that you have never even heard of.

Finally, keep your personal and business accounting separate. If your business ever gets audited, the first thing the IRS looks for is personal expenses disguised as business expenses. A good accountant can help you to know what are legitimate business expenses. Everything you take from the business account, such as payroll and reimbursement, must be recorded and classified.

Being an Employer

Know your situation regarding employees. To begin with, if you have any employees, you will need an Employer Identification Number (EIN), also sometimes called a Federal Tax Identification Number. Getting an EIN is simple: You can fill out IRS form SS-4, or complete the process online at http://www.irs.gov.

Having employees carries other responsibilities and legalities with it. To begin with, you will need to pay payroll taxes (otherwise known as "withholding") to cover income tax, unemployment insurance, Social Security, and Medicare, as well as file W-2 and W-4 forms with the government. You will also be required to pay workman's compensation insurance, and will probably also want to find medical insurance. You are also required to abide by your state's nondiscrimination laws. Most states require you to post nondiscrimination and compensation notices in a public area.

Many employers are tempted to unofficially hire workers "off the books." This can have advantages, but can also mean entering a legal gray area. (Note, however, this is different from hiring freelancers, a temp employed by another company, or having a self-employed professional such as an accountant or bookkeeper come in occasionally to provide a service.) It is one thing to hire the neighbor's teenage son on a one-time basis to help you move some boxes, but quite another to have full-time workers working on a cash-and-carry basis. Regular wages must be noted in the accounts, and gaps may be questioned in the event of an audit. If the workers are injured on the job, you are not covered by workman's comp, and are thus vulnerable to lawsuits. If the workers you hired are not legal residents, you can also be liable for civil and criminal penalties. In general, it is best to keep your employees as above-board as possible.

Building a Business

Good business practices are essential to success. First off, do not overextend yourself. Be honest about what you can do and in what time frame. Secondly, be a responsible business owner. In general, if there is a problem, it is best to explain matters honestly to your clients than to leave them without word and wondering. In the former case, there is at least the possibility of salvaging your reputation and credibility.

Most business is still built by personal contacts and word of mouth. It is for this reason that maintaining your list of contacts is an essential practice. Even if a particular contact may not be useful at a particular moment, a future opportunity may present itself—or you may be able to send someone else to them. Networking, in other words, is as important when you are the boss as when you are looking for a job yourself. As the owner of a company, having a network means getting services on better terms, knowing where to go if you need help with a particular problem, or simply being in the right place at the right time to exploit an opportunity. Join professional organizations, the local Chamber of Commerce, clubs and community organizations, and learn to play golf. And remember—never burn a bridge.

Advertising is another way to build a business. Planning an ad campaign is not as difficult as you might think: You probably already know your media market and business community. The trick is applying it. Again, go with your instincts. If you never look twice at your local weekly, other people probably do not, either. If you are in a high-tourist area, though, local tourists maps might be a good way to leverage your marketing dollar. Ask other people in your area or market who have business similar to your own. Depending on your focus, you might want to consider everything from AM radio or local TV networks, to national trade publications, to hiring a PR firm for an all-out blitz. By thinking about these questions, you can spend your advertising dollars most effectively.

Nor should you underestimate the power of using the Internet to build your business. It is a very powerful tool for small businesses, potentially reaching vast numbers of people for relatively little outlay of money. Launching a Web site has become the modern equivalent of hanging out your shingle. Even if you are primarily a brick-and-mortar business, a Web presence can still be an invaluable tool—your store or offices will show up on Google searches, plus customers can find directions to visit you in person. Furthermore, the Internet offers the small-business owner many useful tools. Print and design services, order fulfillment, credit card processing, and networking—both personal and in terms of linking to other sites—are all available online. Web advertising can be useful, too, either by advertising on specialty sites that appeal to your audience, or by using services such as Google AdWords.

Amateurish print ads, TV commercials, and Web sites do not speak well of your business. Good media should be well-designed, well-edited, and well-put together. It need not, however, be expensive. Shop around and, again, use your network.

Flexibility is also important. "In general, a business must adapt to changing conditions, find new customers and find new products or services that customers need when the demand for their older products or services diminishes," says James Peck, a Long Island, New York, entrepreneur. In other words, if your original plan is not working out, or if demand falls, see if you can parlay your experience, skills, and physical plant into meeting other needs. People are not the only ones who can change their path in life; organizations can, too.

A Final Word

In business, as in other areas of life, the advice of more experienced people is essential. "I think it really takes three businesses until you know what you're doing," Drew Curtis confides. "I sure didn't know what I was doing the first time." Listen to what others have to say, no matter whether it is about your Web site or your business plan. One possible solution is seeking out a mentor, someone who has previously launched a successful venture in this field. In any case, before taking any step, ask as many people as many questions as you can. Good advice is invaluable.

Further Resources

American Independent Business Alliance
http://www.amiba.net

American Small Business League
http://www.asbl.com

IRS Small Business and Self-Employed One-Stop Resource
http://www.irs.gov/businesses/small/index.html

The Riley Guide: Steps in Starting Your Own Business
http://www.rileyguide.com/steps.html

Small Business Administration
http://www.sba.gov

Appendix B

Outfitting Yourself for Career Success

As you contemplate a career shift, the first component is to assess your interests. You need to figure out what makes you tick, since there is a far greater chance that you will enjoy and succeed in a career that taps into your passions, inclinations, natural abilities, and training. If you have a general idea of what your interests are, you at least know in which direction you want to travel. You may know you want to simply switch from one sort of nursing to another, or change your life entirely and pursue a dream you have always held. In this case, you can use a specific volume of The Field Guides to Finding a New Career to discover which position to target. If you are unsure of your direction you want to take, well, then the entire scope of the series is open to you! Browse through to see what appeals to you, and see if it matches with your experience and abilities.

The next step you should take is to make a list—do it once in writing—of the skills you have used in a position of responsibility that transfer to the field you are entering. People in charge of interviewing and hiring may well understand that the skills they are looking for in a new hire are used in other fields, but you must spell it out. Most job descriptions are partly a list of skills. Map your experience into that, and very early in your contacts with a prospective employer explicitly address how you acquired your relevant skills. Pick a relatively unimportant aspect of the job to be your ready answer for where you would look forward to learning within the organization, if this seems essentially correct. When you transfer into a field, softly acknowledge a weakness while relating your readiness to learn, but never lose sight of the value you offer both in your abilities and in the freshness of your perspective.

Energy and Experience

The second component in career-switching success is energy. When Jim Fulmer was 61, he found himself forced to close his piano-repair business. However, he was able to parlay his knowledge of music, pianos, and the musical instruments industry into another job as a sales representative for a large piano manufacturer, and quickly built up a clientele of

127

musical-instrument retailers throughout the East Coast. Fulmer's experience highlights another essential lesson for career-changers: There are plenty of opportunities out there, but jobs will not come to you—especially the career-oriented, well-paying ones. You have to seek them out.

Jim Fulmer's case also illustrates another important point: Former training and experience can be a key to success. "Anyone who has to make a career change in any stage of life has to look at what skills they have acquired but may not be aware of," he says. After all, people can more easily change into careers similar to the ones they are leaving. Training and experience also let you enter with a greater level of seniority, provided you have the other necessary qualifications. For instance, a nurse who is already experienced with administering drugs and their benefits and drawbacks, and who is also graced with the personality and charisma to work with the public, can become a pharmaceutical company sales representative.

Unlock Your Network

The next step toward unlocking the perfect job is networking. The term may be overused, but the idea is as old as civilization. More than other animals, humans need one another. With the Internet and telephone, never in history has it been easier to form (or revive) these essential links. One does not have to gird oneself and attend reunion-type events (though for many this is a fine tactic)—but keep open to opportunities to meet people who may be friendly to you in your field. Ben Franklin understood the principal well—*Poor Richard's Almanac* is something of a treatise on the importance or cultivating what Franklin called "friendships" with benefactors. So follow in the steps of the founding fathers and make friends to get ahead. Remember: helping others feels good; it's often the receiving that gets a little tricky. If you know someone particularly well-connected in your field, consider tapping one or two less important connections first so that you make the most of the important one. As you proceed, keep your strengths foremost in your mind because the glue of commerce is mutual interest.

Eighty percent of job openings are *never advertised*, and, according to the U.S. Bureau of Labor statistics, more than half all employees landed their jobs through networking. Using your personal contacts is far more efficient and effective than trusting your résumé to the Web. On the Web, an employer needs to sort through tens of thousands—or millions—of résumés. When you direct your application to one potential employer, you are directing your inquiry to one person who already knows you. The personal touch is everything: Human beings are social animals, programmed to "read" body language; we are naturally inclined to trust those we meet in person, or who our friends and coworkers have recommended. While Web sites can be useful (for looking through help-wanted ads, for instance), expecting employers to pick you out of the slush pile is as effective as throwing your résumé into a black hole.

Do not send your résumé out just to make yourself feel like you're doing something. The proper way to go about things is to employ discipline and order, and then to apply your charm. Begin your networking efforts by making a list of people you can talk to: colleagues, coworkers, and supervisors, people you have had working relationship with, people from church, athletic teams, political organizations, or other community groups, friends, and relatives. You can expand your networking opportunities by following the suggestions in each chapter of the volumes. Your goal here is not so much to land a job as to expand your possibilities and knowledge: Though the people on your list may not be in the position to help you themselves, they might know someone who is. Meeting with them might also help you understand traits that matter and skills that are valued in the field in which you are interested. Even if the person is a potential employer, it is best to phrase your request as if you were seeking information: "You might not be able to help me, but do you know someone I could talk to who could tell me more about what it is like to work in this field?" Being hungry gives one impression, being desperate quite another.

Keep in mind that networking is a two-way street. If you meet someone who had an opening that is not right for you, but if you could recommend someone else, you have just added to your list two people who will be favorably disposed toward you in the future. Also, bear in mind that *you* can help people in *your* old field, thus adding to your own contacts list.

Networking is especially important to the self-employed or those who start their own businesses. Many people in this situation begin because they either recognize a potential market in a field that they are familiar with, or because full-time employment in this industry is no longer a possibility. Already being well-established in a field can help, but so can asking connections for potential work and generally making it known that you are ready, willing, and able to work. Working your professional connections, in many cases, is the *only* way to establish yourself. A freelancer's network, in many cases, is like a spider's web. The spider casts out many strands, since he or she never knows which one might land the next meal.

Dial-Up Help

In general, it is better to call contacts directly than to e-mail them. E-mails are easy for busy people to ignore or overlook, even if they do not mean to. Explain your situation as briefly as possible (see the discussion of the "elevator speech"), and ask if you could meet briefly, either at their office or at a neutral place such as a café. (Be sure that you pay the bill in such a situation—it is a way of showing you appreciate their time and effort.) If you get someone's voicemail, give your "elevator speech" and then say you will call back in a few days to follow up—and then do so. If you reach your contact directly and they are too busy to speak or meet with you, make a definite appointment to call back at a later date. Be persistent, but not annoying.

Once you have arranged a meeting, prep yourself. Look at industry publications both in print and online, as well as news reports (here, GoogleNews, which lets you search through online news reports, can be very handy). Having up-to-date information on industry trends shows that you are dedicated, knowledgeable, and focused. Having specific questions on employers and requests for suggestions will set you apart from the rest of the job-hunting pack. Knowing the score—for instance, asking about the value of one sort of certification instead of another— pegs you as an "insider," rather than a dilettante, someone whose name is worth remembering and passing along to a potential employer.

Finally, set the right mood. Here, a little self-hypnosis goes a long way: Look at yourself in the mirror, and tell yourself that you are an enthusiastic, committed professional. Mood affects confidence and performance. Discipline your mind so you keep your perspective and self-respect. Nobody wants to hire someone who comes across as insincere, tells a sob story, or is still in the doldrums of having lost their previous job. At the end of any networking meeting, ask for someone else who might be able to help you in your journey to finding a position in this field, either with information or a potential job opening.

Get a Lift

When you meet with a contact in person (as well as when you run into anyone by chance who may be able to help you), you need an "elevator speech" (so-named because it should be short enough to be delivered during an elevator ride from a ground level to a high floor). This is a summary in which, in less than two minutes, you give them a clear impression of who you are, where you come from, your experience and goals, and why you are on the path you are on. The motto above Plato's Academy holds true: Know Thyself (this is where our Career Compasses and guides will help you). A long and rambling "elevator story" will get you nowhere. Furthermore, be positive: Neither a sad-sack story nor a tirade explaining how everything that went wrong in your old job is someone else's fault will get you anywhere. However, an honest explanation of a less-than-fortunate circumstance, such as a decline in business forcing an office closing, needing to change residence to a place where you are not qualified to work in order to further your spouse's career, or needing to work fewer hours in order to care for an ailing family member, is only honest.

An elevator speech should show 1) you know the business involved; 2) you know the company; 3) you are qualified (here, try to relate your education and work experience to the new situation); and 4) you are goal-oriented, dependable, and hardworking. Striking a balance is important; you want to sound eager, but not overeager. You also want to show a steady work experience, but not that you have been so narrowly focused that you cannot adjust. Most important is emphasizing what you can do for the company. You will be surprised how much information you can include in two minutes. Practice this speech in front of a mirror until you have the key points down perfectly. It should sound natural, and you should come across as friendly, confident, and assertive. Finally, remember eye contact! Good eye contact needs to be part of your presentation, as well as your everyday approach when meeting potential employers and leads.

Get Your Résumé Ready

Everyone knows what a résumé is, but how many of us have really thought about how to put one together? Perhaps no single part of the job search is subject to more anxiety—or myths and misunderstandings—than this 8 ½-by-11-inch sheet of paper.

On the one hand, it is perfectly all right for someone—especially in certain careers, such as academia—to have a résumé that is more than one page. On the other hand, you do not need to tell a future employer *everything*. Trim things down to the most relevant; for a 40-year-old to mention an internship from two decades ago is superfluous. Likewise, do not include irrelevant jobs, lest you seem like a professional career-changer.

Tailor your descriptions of your former employment to the particular position you are seeking. This is not to say you should lie, but do make your experience more appealing. If the job you're looking for involves supervising other people, say if you have done this in the past; if it involves specific knowledge or capabilities, mention that you possess these qualities. In general, try to make your past experience seem as similar to what you are seeking.

The standard advice is to put your Job Objective at the heading of the résumé. An alternative to this is a Professional Summary, which some recruiters and employers prefer. The difference is that a Job Objective mentions the position you are seeking, whereas a Professional Summary mentions your background (e.g. "Objective: To find a position as a sales representative in agribusiness machinery" versus "Experienced sales representative; strengths include background in agribusiness, as well as building team dynamics and market expansion"). Of course, it is easy to come up with two or three versions of the same document for different audiences.

The body of the résumé of an experienced worker varies a lot more than it does at the beginning of your career. You need not put your education or your job experience first; rather, your résumé should emphasize your strengths. If you have a master's degree in a related field, that might want to go before your unrelated job experience. Conversely, if too much education will harm you, you might want to bury that under the section on professional presentations you have given that show how good you are at communicating. If you are currently enrolled in a course or other professional development, be sure to note this (as well as your date of expected graduation). A résumé is a study of blurs, highlights, and jewels. You blur everything you must in order to fit the description of your experience to the job posting. You highlight what is relevant from each and any of your positions worth mentioning. The jewels are the little headers and such—craft them, since they are what is seen first.

You may also want to include professional organizations, work-related achievements, and special abilities, such as your fluency in a foreign language. Also mention your computer software qualifications and capabilities, especially if you are looking for work in a technological field or if you are an older job-seeker who might be perceived as behind the technology curve. Including your interests or family information might or might not be a good idea—no one really cares about your bridge club, and in fact they might worry that your marathon training might take away from your work commitments, but, on the other hand, mentioning your golf handicap or three children might be a good idea if your potential employer is an avid golfer or is a family woman herself.

You can either include your references or simply note, "References available upon request." However, be sure to ask your references' permission to use their names and alert them to the fact that they may be contacted before you include them on your résumé! Be sure to include name, organization, phone number, and e-mail address for each contact.

Today, word processors make it easy to format your résumé. However, beware of prepackaged résumé "wizards"—they do not make you stand out in the crowd. Feel free to strike out on your own, but remember the most important thing in formatting a résumé is consistency. Unless you have a background in typography, do not get too fancy. Finally, be sure to have someone (or several people!) read your résumé over for you.

For more information on résumé writing, check out Web sites such as http://www.resume.monster.com.

Craft Your Cover Letter

It is appropriate to include a cover letter with your résumé. A cover letter lets you convey extra information about yourself that does not fit or is not always appropriate in your résumé, such as why you are no longer working in your original field of employment. You can and should also mention the name of anyone who referred you to the job. You can go into some detail about the reason you are a great match, given the job description. Also address any questions that might be raised in the potential employer's mind (for instance, a gap in employment). Do not, however, ramble on. Your cover letter should stay focused on your goal: To offer a strong, positive impression of yourself and persuade the hiring manager that you are worth an interview. Your cover letter gives you a chance to stand out from the other applicants and sell yourself. In fact, according to a CareerBuilder.com survey, 23 percent of hiring managers say a candidate's ability to relate his or her experience to the job at hand is a top hiring consideration.

Even if you are not a great writer, you can still craft a positive yet concise cover letter in three paragraphs: An introduction containing the specifics of the job you are applying for; a summary of why you are a good fit for the position and what you can do for the company; and a closing with a request for an interview, contact information, and thanks. Remember to vary the structure and tone of your cover letter—do not begin every sentence with "I."

Ace Your Interview

In truth, your interview begins well before you arrive. Be sure to have read up well on the company and its industry. Use Web sites and magazines—http://www.hoovers.com offers free basic business information, and trade magazines deliver both information and a feel for the industries they cover. Also, do not neglect talking to people in your circle who might know about trends in the field. Leave enough time to digest the information so that you can give some independent thought to the company's history and prospects. You don't need to expert when you arrive to be interviewed; but you should be comfortable. The most important element of all is to be poised and relaxed during the interview itself. Preparation and practice can help a lot.

Be sure to develop well-thought-through answers to the following, typical interview openers and standard questsions.

☞ Tell me about yourself. (Do not complain about how unsatisfied you were in your former career, but give a brief summary

of your applicable background and interest in the particular job area.) If there is a basis to it, emphasize how much
you love to work and how you are a team player.

☞ Why do you want this job? (Speak from the brain, and the heart—of
course you want the money, but say a little here about what you
find interesting about the field and the company's role in it.)

☞ What makes you a good hire? (Remember here to connect the
company's needs and your skill set. Ultimately, your selling
points probably come down to one thing: you will make your employer money. You want the prospective hirer to see that your
skills are valuable not to the world in general but to this specific company's bottom line. What can you do for them?)

☞ What led you to leave your last job? (If you were fired, still try say
something positive, such as, "The business went through a challenging time, and some of the junior marketing people were let go.")

Practice answering these and other questions, and try to be genuinely positive about yourself, and patient with the process. Be secure but
not cocky; don't be shy about forcing the focus now and then on positive
contributions you have made in your working life—just be specific. As
with the elevator speech, practice in front of the mirror.

A couple pleasantries are as natural a way as any to start the actual
interview, but observe the interviewer closely for any cues to fall silent
and formally begin. Answer directly; when in doubt, finish your phrase
and look to the interviewer. Without taking command, you can always
ask, "Is there more you would like to know?" Your attentiveness will convey respect. Let your personality show too—a positive attitude and a
grounded sense of your abilities will go a long way to getting you considered. During the interview, keep your cell phone off and do not look at
your watch. Toward the end of your meeting, you may be asked whether
you have any questions. It is a good idea to have one or two in mind. A
few examples follow:

☞ "What makes your company special in the field?"
☞ "What do you consider the hardest part of this position?"
☞ "Where are your greatest opportunities for growth?"
☞ "Do you know when you might need anything further from me?"

Leave discussion of terms for future conversations. Make a cordial, smooth exit.

Remember to Follow Up

Send a thank-you note. Employers surveyed by CareerBuilder.com in 2005 said it matters. About 15 percent said they would not hire someone who did not follow up with a thanks. And almost 33 percent would think less of a candidate. The form of the note does not much matter—if you know a manager's preference, use it. Otherwise, just be sure to follow up.

Winning an Offer

A job offer can feel like the culmination of a long and difficult struggle. So naturally, when you hear them, you may be tempted to jump at the offer. Don't. Once an employer wants you, he or she will usually give you a chance to consider the offer. This is the time to discuss terms of employment, such as vacation, overtime, and benefits. A little effort now can be well worth it in the future. Be sure to do a check of prevailing salaries for your field and area before signing on. Web sites for this include Payscale.com, Salary.com, and Salaryexpert.com. If you are thinking about asking for better or different terms from what the prospective employer offered, rest assured—that's how business gets done; and it may just burnish the positive impression you have already made.

Index